In Pursuit

*Go After What You Want -
Alive, Aligned, and Fully You*

Jessica Smarro

Published by Project ICON

Paperback ISBN: 978-1-969888-15-1
Hardcover ISBN: 978-1-969888-14-4

https://projecticon.io/

Table of Contents

Introduction

The Real Pursuit

What if the point of your life wasn't to get "there" as fast as possible, but to savor every twist and turn of becoming? What if the prize isn't achieving the goal, the applause, or even that picture-perfect life on paper, but instead the version of you that awakens each day, ever-evolving and resilient? These opening lines present a clear challenge: to experience life in its fullness, to cherish the messy unfolding of who you are becoming, and to recognize that every step, every stumble, and every triumph is a sacred part of the journey.

This book isn't about doing more, fixing yourself, or finally becoming "enough." It is an invitation to become more of who you truly are, deliberately and wholeheartedly. It offers a call to break the cycle of constant proving, relentless performing, and endless perfecting. It asks you to learn how to chase big dreams without sacrificing the essence of your being. Too often, the frantic pace of achievement causes us to forget that every moment carries a lesson in self-discovery. You've probably done all the "right" things: built a résumé, earned degrees, climbed career ladders, nurtured relationships, and even started your healing journey. And yet, despite all of this, a quiet whisper may still remain, asking the same haunting question: *Why doesn't this feel like freedom?*

If that question resonates, then this book is for you.

The Journey You're About to Take

This is not another run-of-the-mill productivity pep talk or a superficial mindset makeover. This is a recalibration—a gentle yet resolute return to your inner compass, long obscured by a maze of expectations, achievements, and the pursuit of external validation. Within these pages, you will discover how to identify and dismantle the invisible prisons of perfectionism, the chains of people-pleasing, and the ceaseless demands to perform. You will be guided through practical tools, such as the

S.T.E.A.R. model for managing thoughts and emotions, and the F.R.E.E. framework for rebuilding emotional safety and self-trust. The journey is both an inward exploration and a creative reimagining of what success truly means when it emanates from your core rather than from external accolades.

This isn't merely a book to be read. It is a dynamic conversation, an intimate coaching session, a call to return home to the self that lies beneath all the noise. Real-life practices, reflection prompts, and raw, unfiltered stories from my journey and others who have walked similar paths will guide you in applying these insights in real time. The process is not about waiting for that perfect "someday" moment. Instead, it is about embracing every goal, challenge, obstacle, and experience as an opportunity for increased awareness, growth, evolution, and expansion.

Why I Wrote This Book
I wrote this book as a message to my younger self, a bit of a love letter if you will, to the version of me who spent years chasing peace through performance. I wrote this book for the 7-year-old girl who, despite not feeling safe in her own home, still summoned the courage to show up for herself, for the adult woman who, despite ticking every box and doing everything "right," felt an unyielding inner void. I also wrote it for those who find themselves silently questioning, *What's wrong with me if I still feel empty after all I've achieved? Why does it seem as though I'm merely performing life rather than living it? And what if, in slowing down, I don't lose my edge but instead finally discover my authentic self?* This isn't theory. I've lived it. I've left the good-on-paper marriage. Walked away from the prestigious job. Smashed the glass bowls in the basement out of grief and rage. Slowly and deliberately, I built a life I actually want to be inside of—not one that looks perfect, but one that feels like home.

I'm not writing this book as a guru, expert, or someone who has it all figured out. I'm writing it as someone who is still in it. Someone who has stumbled, spiraled, stood back up, and kept walking. I've figured out some things that have made a real difference in my life and in the lives of the hundreds of clients I've worked with, and I want to share those things with you, not as gospel, but as an invitation. Take what lands. Leave what doesn't. This book is not a prescription. It's a conversation. If anything I share helps you feel less alone, more seen, or a little more free, then that's everything I hoped for when I put these words on the page.

What to Expect

As you journey through this book, you will traverse transformative shifts. You will learn to see the invisible patterns that have kept you stuck and gain powerful tools to interrupt the mental loops that drain your energy. Along the way, you will cultivate the emotional fluency necessary to trust yourself again, to redefine success not by external standards but by the truth that resides within you.

Each chapter combines honest conversation with practical tools. My hope is not just to give you an engaging and thought-provoking book, but also to offer a roadmap for transformation, an invitation to show up in your life with purpose and passion. By the time you turn the final page, you will understand why your previous pursuit patterns didn't lead to lasting fulfillment, and you will hold in your hands a new map and a redefined compass. A compass that points not toward an ever-elusive finish line, but toward the ongoing, sacred dance of life, a pursuit rooted in wholeness rather than hustle.

The truth is, the destination will feel like the journey, so don't postpone the experience you want to have until you get to the "finish line." You get to experience a journey that feels like freedom, fulfillment, satisfaction.

Are you ready?

Let's begin.

Before you begin, download your companion worksheet: *The Prison, The Path, The Pursuit.*
Use it to get honest, get clear, and take the next bold step toward a life that feels alive, aligned, and fully you.

PART I:

THE PRISON

Seeing What's Keeping You Stuck

Chapter 1:

When the Finish Line Isn't Freedom

The Myth of Arrival: Why Chasing "There" Never Feels Like Enough

A few years ago, I was sitting in a packed ballroom with over a thousand other coaches. The energy was electric. Imagine Tony Robbins meets a TED Talk with a Beyoncé halftime show vibe. We clapped, cried, and celebrated the people who were reaching six-, seven-, even eight-figure businesses. I know, I know... my inner cool girl is rolling her eyes too. But hear me out. As much as these amped-up conferences make great fodder for cult jokes and parody skits (and believe me, they do), there is something undeniably powerful about being in a room full of humans who are genuinely trying to access their highest selves, shake off old stories, stop playing small, and build something that matters.

One woman took the stage, glowing and eight months pregnant, her round belly unmistakable. She shared how she hit her million-dollar milestone. It was the thing she had dreamed about for years. She said she expected confetti and champagne. Instead, she picked up the phone, called her best friend, and sobbed. Her words to her bestie hit me like a punch to the chest.

"But why am I still me?"

Oof.

She thought that number would transform her. She thought it would alchemize her into someone who no longer second-guessed herself. She assumed she'd become someone who didn't spiral into doubt or shame or insecurity. But she hit the goal and... she was still her, still carrying the ache, still carrying the belief that she wasn't quite enough. Why? Because the destination will always feel like the journey. You will not magically feel different and be different simply because you've achieved an arbitrary goal.

That moment echoed so many of my own. Graduation day. The performance review. Speaking on a national stage. I thought each one would click something into place. But they didn't. I was still me. And for a long time, I didn't know what to do with that disappointment.

So, what do we tend to do?

We chase again. We chase harder. We call it ambition, but it's escape. It's escape from sitting with the parts of ourselves that feel incomplete unless something shiny is happening. It's an escape from asking harder questions like: *"What if I stopped running long enough to actually feel my life?"*

It got me thinking about how often we find ourselves sprinting toward some version of "there," like it's the promised land. Like it holds the missing piece to our peace, the final key to our confidence, the reason we'll finally be able to breathe. It's as if, once we hit the goal, whatever that goal is, we'll finally arrive in our own life. We'll get to exhale, let our shoulders drop, and finally feel the quiet relief of being enough.

Except… it never quite happens that way.

"There" is slippery. You land the job, and now you're eyeing the promotion. You hit the revenue goal, but now it has to be scalable. You lose the weight, but now it's about tone, or maintenance, or your arms under fluorescent lighting. And don't even get me started on social media. When your feed becomes your scoreboard, self-worth gets handed over to likes, views, and algorithmic applause. You start measuring the richness of your life against curated highlight reels, forgetting that filters are not facts.

This, my friend, is what I call *Arrival Addiction*. It's sneaky. It's socially celebrated. And it is exhausting.

Arrival Addiction is what happens when we mistake achievement for identity. When we've absorbed the message that worth must be earned, that hustle equals value, and that peace is a prize reserved for the ones who checked enough boxes. It's burnout gospel wrapped in productivity language. It sells because it sounds noble, driven, and growth-minded. But far too often, it isn't about drive. It's about avoidance. We're not chasing the goal. We're chasing the *feeling* we believe the goal will finally unlock.

9

We dress it up with vision boards and to-do lists. We call it strategy, but beneath the color-coded calendar is often something much quieter. We're avoiding the ache. The ache of loneliness. The ache of grief. The ache of uncertainty. The ache of sitting still with a version of ourselves we're not sure how to love without an achievement attached.

So, we stay busy. We perform wholeness. We curate ambition. We chase the next iteration of ourselves, not because we're enamored with the future, but because we're not sure how to sit with the present. We confuse motion with meaning and achievement with aliveness. Chronic pursuit becomes our coping mechanism.

In Pursuit Insight: Arrival Addiction is chasing peace you already have. You don't become enough by arriving. When you stop running and come home to yourself, you remember you always were.

And because Arrival Addiction wears ambition's costume, it's easy to miss. But underneath the glow-up fantasy, the perfectly timed morning routine, the visionary business plan, and the aesthetic life is often something much less glamorous: self-abandonment.

The real truth is, you cannot heal what you're not willing to feel. I know that sounds like a bumper sticker, but it's true. You can't feel at home in a life you're constantly rushing through. Arrival Addiction whispers that if you just keep going, if you just try harder, it'll all click into place. But it rarely does. Instead, we get stuck in the loop. We check the box and create a new one. Then we hit the goal and feel... nothing. Or worse, feel like a fraud.

The lie that Arrival Addiction sells is that the next achievement will finally fix the ache. But the ache is not caused by a lack of success; it comes from disconnection. We become disconnected from our bodies, from our desires, from the present moment, and from the deeper truth that we are already whole, even without external proof.

Arrival Addiction says, *you'll feel free when you get there.* But the truth is, you'll only feel free when you learn how to feel free *here*.

I want to be clear. I'm not anti-goal. I'm not here to tell you to shrink your dreams or quiet your ambition. Quite the opposite. I love big vision energy. I love the thrill of a new idea, the sprint toward something meaningful, pushing the envelope of what you think is possible for you. YES. TO. ALL. OF. THAT.

But here is the difference: when pursuit turns into performance and becomes a way to hide from your feelings, it stops being about expansion and starts being about avoidance.

If you don't feel whole on the way there, you won't feel whole when you arrive. Peace doesn't wait at the finish line; it lives inside you. And the more you practice presence, the more you remember that truth.

Real fulfillment isn't found in the next win. It's built in the present, born in the ordinary moments when you choose to stay, choose to feel, and stop outsourcing your worth and start anchoring into it.

I think the ache inside you isn't failure. I think of it as feedback. It's something inside of you saying, *"I'm ready for something deeper."* Not shinier. Not more impressive. Just more true, more expansive, and more you.

So, if you've ever looked around your life and thought, *"I did everything they said to do, and I still feel off,"* I want you to hear this: you're not broken. You're just waking up to the realization that all those achievements and all those gold stars never quite filled the space you hoped they would. And that's okay, because they were never meant to.

What you've been chasing isn't wrong. It just isn't the whole story. The good news is, you don't have to burn it all down to write a new one. You just have to stop running from the chapter you're in.

Compass Check:
- What are you chasing right now, and why?
- What do you believe it will give you?
- What would it look like to start practicing peace, fulfillment, pride, satisfaction (or whatever you think waits for you at the goal line) now, instead of waiting until later?

This week, choose one moment each day to stop doing and start feeling, even if it feels awkward. Actually, *especially* if it feels awkward. That's how you start building a life that truly feels like home.

Life on Paper, Numb in the Mirror: Checking Boxes but Feeling Empty

You could say I come from a non-traditional background. I don't mean that in the cute, quirky, rom-com kind of way. I mean it in the statistical *"you're not supposed to make it out"* kind of way. By all accounts, I wasn't supposed to be here, doing this work or living this version of life.

I was born to a single, teenage mother addicted to meth. My earliest memories of family gatherings aren't holiday traditions or family dinners with "tell me your peak and valley of the day"–style conversations. My family memories are peppered with collect calls from jail. I remember one holiday in particular, turkey in the oven, mashed potatoes on the stove, and a cordless phone making its way around the table. Each aunt, uncle, and cousin took their turn calling in from their respective correctional facility. The background noise wasn't laughter or music. It was the flat tone of a prison phone system: *"This is a collect call from an inmate at…"*

Merry Christmas from Unit C.

Even back then, when I was still small enough to need a stepstool to reach the sink, I knew that this wasn't going to be my story. It wasn't because I was "better." It wasn't because I had some superior moral compass. It was simply because something in me whispered, gently but relentlessly, *this isn't it. This isn't who you're here to be.*

I didn't have the language for it yet, but that spark, that knowing, was the beginning of my pursuit. It was not the pursuit of applause or success or shiny Instagram-worthy milestones that called to me. Just… *more*. More than survival. More than inherited chaos. More than the exhausting effort of keeping my head above water in a current I didn't choose.

So, I did what so many high-functioning, high-achieving, hyper-adaptive kids do when chaos becomes the backdrop of their lives: I picked up the Rule Book.

You know the one.

Get good grades. Go to college. Choose a safe major. Get a good job. Marry someone stable. Be kind. Be agreeable. Don't ask for too much. Smile in the photos. Be proud but not arrogant. Be smart but not intimidating. Have the babies (after the wedding, of course), and decorate the house in warm neutrals from the seasonal aisle at Target.

Check. Check. Check.

I became really good at checking boxes... well, maybe not the home decor part, but... I became a professional rule-follower. Valedictorian. First in my family to go to college. Graduated *summa cum laude*. Then came the grad degree, the paid internship, the job that looked incredible on LinkedIn. Traveled to D.C., sat in meetings at the White House, and was nominated Person of the Year. Married the good-on-paper man—the sweet, steady, responsible one with the loyal family and the reliable laugh.

And here's the thing: I was proud. I still am. I worked hard. I earned those moments. I made a life that, on paper, was a picture of the American Dream. I escaped the chaos. I outran the narrative. I broke the cycle.

But inside... everything was grayscale.

I used to describe it to close friends like, *"It's like I'm living a half-lived life, everything's in black and white."* Like I'm watching my own life play out from behind glass. Technically, nothing is wrong. Everything looks fine. But something essential is missing.

And no, there was no dramatic rock bottom. No cinematic breakdown. Just this persistent, low-humming numbness. Like a melody I couldn't quite catch. A quiet sense that maybe I'd followed all the rules and still wound up in the wrong story.

The difficult period wasn't rooted in circumstances being objectively bad. As a child, I'd survey my surroundings and think, *"This is wrong; something has to change."* But that black-and-white phase wasn't "bad" in the conventional sense. It appeared right, even proper. Yet it felt anything but. There was no sense of fulfillment. No vitality. Life was happening around me, but I wasn't connected to it. I was excelling at a version of life that made sense on paper, but left me wondering why it still felt off.

There's a quote I've always loved by Joseph Campbell: *"If the path before you is clear, you're probably on someone else's."* And let me tell you, my path was clear. It had a four-year plan, a 401(k), and a procreation plan that neatly lined up with my then-husband's PhD dissertation schedule. But… I didn't feel fully alive.

That's the tricky thing about socially acceptable success. You can follow every rule, tick every box, and still feel like a ghost in your own skin. You can still find yourself sitting in your car during your commute, staring out the windshield, thinking, *Is this it? Is this what I worked so hard for?*

We call it success, but it felt like sleepwalking.

That's what happens when achievement replaces alignment. When we become so skilled at meeting expectations that we forget to check in with ourselves. When the story we're living no longer matches the voice inside, whispering something truer, deeper, and more alive.

What I need you to hear is that I wasn't broken, and neither are you. What I was experiencing wasn't failure. It was an awakening. A sacred kind of unrest that asks, *"What if this isn't the only version of your life available to you?"*

It's tempting, in those moments, to panic and assume the only way forward is to blow it all up. Quit the job. Leave the relationship. Sell the house. Start fresh. And sometimes, yes, you do that. But other times, it starts with one quiet act of honesty with yourself. It doesn't have to be dramatic or reckless, just honest.

You need to get honest about what fits in your life and what doesn't. You need to be honest about what brings you to life and what makes you feel like you're disappearing. You also need to be honest about which parts of your life were built from love, alignment, and joy, and which ones were built from obligation, fear, or survival strategies you learned long before you knew you had a choice. This isn't about fixing you. This is about finding you.

And no, that doesn't mean moving to Bali or chanting affirmations under a fig tree (although it could). It means noticing. It means listening. It means giving yourself enough stillness to hear the stories you're telling yourself and asking: *Do these stories actually feel true? Are they helping me become more alive, more connected, more me?*

For me, the thought that kept circling my brain was: *"I've done everything 'right.' So why doesn't this feel the way I thought it would?"*

The reason is that success without self-connection isn't really success. It's empty.

And I didn't want an empty life. I wanted a *felt* one. A *full* one.

Eventually, I made some changes. Some of them were small, some seismic. But the most powerful shift wasn't in my relationship status, my zip code, or my job title. It was in my posture toward my own joy. I stopped outsourcing my life to what was on the list. I stopped waiting for a milestone to grant me permission to feel good, and I started asking questions like, *"What would it look like to build a life that feels good to live, not just to look at?"*
These are the kinds of questions that had me coming home to myself.

In Pursuit Insight:
A life that looks perfect on paper but feels numb in your body isn't a failure. It's feedback. It's your soul tugging on your sleeve, saying, *"I'm ready to be seen again."* When you stop measuring success by someone else's rulebook and start reconnecting to your voice, joy, and truth, you begin to trade performance for presence and that's where the real magic lives.

And that's the invitation I want to extend to you. It's not an invitation to torch the life you've built. It's about asking yourself, gently and honestly: *Does this reflect me? Is this mine? Does this feel like a life I want to be inside of?*

You weren't made to live a life that only makes sense to other people.
You were made to live a life that feels like *you*. Lit up. Messy. Awake. Honest.

And no, not every moment will be euphoric. Sometimes being present to your own life means sitting in discomfort, holding tension, grieving the things that didn't turn out the way you hoped. But at least it's real. At least it's *yours*.

Compass Check:
- Where in your life are you checking boxes instead of checking in?
- What parts of your life feel built from fear or obligation?
- What would it look like to make one small choice this week that's rooted in your joy instead of your résumé?

You don't have to burn it all down to build something beautiful. You just have to begin by telling yourself the truth.

Rewriting the Goal of the Goal: From Outcomes to Becoming

When I was a kid, I had a goal of revolutionizing the prison systems of America. You know, just your typical childhood dream. While other kids were plotting ways to become astronauts or pop stars, I was brainstorming how to restructure incarceration. Looking back, I can't help but smile at that version of me. She was so earnest, so intense, so convinced that if she could just fix the system, she could save the people she loved.

Turns out, the real revolution wasn't what I thought it was. It wasn't about changing policy, reworking programs, or writing a better inmate handbook. It was about helping people, including myself, break free from the prison of an unmanaged mind.

Of course, I didn't have that language back then. I just saw my family cycling in and out of jail, bouncing between courtrooms and correctional facilities, always promising that this time would be different. Only it never was. I remember watching that pattern and thinking, *This isn't working. Something about this has to change.* And in my child-brain logic, I decided that if I could change the system, I could change their lives. And if I could change their lives, then maybe I'd finally feel like everything was okay.

Flash forward to six months after grad school. I found myself scrolling job listings, still carrying that same torch for justice reform, and boom, there it was. A listing for the Johnson County Jail Alternatives Program.

It was like Craigslist had sent out a bat signal just for me. Here was my shot. My chance to be the change. And I took it.

I spent nearly fifteen years working within that system, running programs, creating pathways, and designing diversion strategies to interrupt incarceration cycles. And some of it was revolutionary. I got to do meaningful work at the intersection of people and policy; but the deeper lesson was that systems are made of humans. And most humans, whether they're incarcerated, employed by the institutions, or writing the policies that govern them, are not trained in how to be with themselves. They don't understand their operating system. They don't know how to partner with their brain. They don't know how to navigate the inner terrain of thoughts, feelings, and behaviors. They're lost in their loops, just like the people they're trying to "rehabilitate."

Those experiences shifted my focus to a new mission—one rooted not in policy, but in personal liberation. The next wave of revolution wasn't about cells and statutes. It was about consciousness. The prison I wanted to help people escape wasn't built with bars. It was built with beliefs, thoughts, fears, and unexamined patterns running on autopilot. The real work was about teaching people how to navigate their own minds, instead of being trapped inside them.

And a key part of that liberation is rewriting our relationship with goals.

In high school and college, goals were simple. Finish the assignment. Get the A. Then, and only then, can you rest, enjoy, and relax. I wasn't there to learn. I was there to win. My focus was to cross the finish line as fast as possible and collect whatever validation came with it.

But in my thirties, something shifted. I started to wonder... *What if the goal isn't just to "get it right"? What if the real goal is to be self-honoring?*

That shift came into focus when I walked into my boss's office, an elected sheriff, and told him I was resigning. After nearly fifteen years in the justice system, I was moving 1,100 miles away. For a boy. His exact response, delivered with a mix of disbelief and disgust, was, *"Sounds like you're making this decision with your heart, not your head."*

To which I smiled and said, *"Exactly."*

That moment mattered. It wasn't just about leaving a job. It was about choosing a different compass. It was about choosing to set goals from the inside out, from connection and presence. It was about setting goals from my full self.

When I turned 40, I got a tattoo on my wrist that says "Be Here Now" in Sanskrit. Allegedly. I don't actually read Sanskrit, so we're all trusting the tattoo artist and Google Translate on this one. Still, that phrase became a north star for me. It serves as a reminder that the most powerful place to set goals isn't from lack, but from presence and being fully in the here and now.

Too often, we set goals as escape hatches. We're unhappy, so we chase more money. We feel invisible, so we seek validation through achievement. We feel insecure, so we set a goal to "finally get in shape." But as we explored with Arrival Addiction, chasing a goal to fix how we feel is a setup. We're outsourcing our emotional life to a finish line that can't deliver. All of our emotions, including happiness, worth, adequacy, and peace, are generated by our thoughts. They are not waiting for us in the future. They are available now, or not at all.

In Pursuit Insight: You don't set goals because you're incomplete. You set them because you're ready to expand. To discover new parts of your capacity. Goals wake up the dormant brilliance inside you. Not because you weren't enough before, but because now you're ready to remember more of who you are.

The purpose of goals isn't to make us happier, more complete, or more fulfilled. That's our mind's job.

The purpose of goals is *evolution*.

Goals are doorways. They invite us into new parts of ourselves. They don't complete us. They reveal us. They stretch us into corners we didn't know we had.

Lean in closer for what I'm about to say. Achieving your goals won't make you better. It won't make you more deserving. It won't make you enough. Because you already are.

What the pursuit of your goal *will* do is strip away the stuff that blocks your awareness of that truth. It will challenge your conditioning. It will confront your self-imposed limits. It will reveal what's been buried under years of proving, pleasing, and performing.

The old way of setting goals sounds like this:

Make a million dollars so I can finally feel safe.
Lose the weight so I can feel confident.
Be chosen so I can feel seen.
Get the promotion so I can feel worthy.
Get the house/life/Instagram aesthetic so I can feel in control.

But there's another way.

What if your goals weren't desperation plays from a place of lack, but bold declarations of aliveness from a place of wholeness? What if you permitted yourself to *want*, not because something is missing, but because something inside you is ready to grow?

Try this with me.

Write down 15 things you want. It can be anything. A dream home. A beach vacation. More intimacy. A thriving business. Write it all down.

Now look at your list. How many of those things do you already have? If the answer is zero, don't shame yourself. Most people create goals from scarcity. We're taught to. But let's try again.

Now rewrite your list with a new rhythm. This time, alternate between something you want that you already have and something you want that you don't yet have. Keep that pattern going by alternating one you have and one you don't until you've named 15 things.

Maybe it's your home. Your favorite coffee mug. The way your partner rubs your back without asking. Describe each thing in detail. Let yourself feel the goodness of it.

Now, when you name the next thing you want, feel the difference. Notice how it lands. Feel the difference when your desire is rooted in gratitude instead of grasping.

You've just made what I call an *abundance sandwich*.

It's a simple but powerful way to remember that fulfillment is not a reward waiting at the end of the race. It's something you can experience right now.

And from that place, your goals become less about *escape* and more about *expression*.

Compass Check:
- Where are you setting goals from a sense of lack instead of a sense of wholeness?
- What would it look like to set a goal from a place of abundance, presence, and curiosity?

Try the "abundance sandwich" this week. Notice how it changes your energy, your desires, your clarity. You don't have to wait until you arrive to feel alive. You can start now.

Chapter 2:

The Invisible Prisons We Live In

Performing, Pleasing, Perfecting: How High Achievers Self-Abandon

Let's play a game. Think back to the first memory you have where you realized that "being good" or "getting it right" got you something you needed: love, approval, or safety.
I'll go first.

When I was nine, I moved from Amarillo, Texas, to a tiny town in Iowa. Population 1,900. I knew exactly five people: my aunt, uncle, and their three kids. Yes, the same aunt from the "collect calls from jail" story. Naturally, I stuck close to my cousins and their crew because that's who I knew.

On one of the first days at my new school, we were out at recess on a playground with a giant wooden castle, monkey bars that burned your palms, and mulch that got stuck in your shoes. Two girls approached me. They had that confidence that kids either inherit or sharpen young. One of them looked me straight in the eye and said, "The boys think you're cute, so you should hang out with us instead of those girls."

That was the first time I remember outsourcing my authority.

I didn't have the language for it then, but that was the moment I understood something important. Someone out there makes the rules. Someone else decides what's cool, who's worthy, and what's acceptable. And if I want to belong, I'd better align myself with whoever's holding that invisible rulebook.

The message was clear. Don't trust yourself. Default to what others think. Follow their cues, not your own knowing.

Of course, that's a slippery slope. Fast forward a few years, when those same boys no longer thought I fit the "cute" criteria, the same girls who had once offered me a golden ticket wanted nothing to do with me. The message only grew stronger. Be what's palatable. Be who they want. Or be left behind.

That's the birthplace of self-abandonment, and it usually starts young. Maybe for you, it was on a playground. Maybe it began in a living room. It could have started with your parents, your peers, your pastor, or your first love. It often begins as something small, almost invisible. You choose the "right" friends. You wear the "right" jeans with the flashiest back-pocket patch. You laugh at a joke that made you uncomfortable. You start turning parts of yourself up or down depending on who is in the room.

It may look harmless, even adaptable. But these tiny shape-shifts, the self-edits made in the name of approval, begin to add up. When repeated over time, they create something much heavier. You start to lose track of where you end and where someone else begins. And most of the time, you don't even realize it's happening.

Let's talk about self-abandonment, not as a concept, but as a lived experience. It happens when you stop consulting yourself about your own life. It happens when you override your own instincts, silence your needs, and shrink your desires because somewhere along the way, you learned that someone else's comfort, preferences, or opinions mattered more than your own.

It looks like saying yes when your soul is screaming no. It shows up as apologizing for things that weren't your fault, or apologizing for existing altogether. You know the move, someone bumps into you in an overcrowded Costco aisle, and you say sorry. It looks like silencing yourself in meetings to appear agreeable. It presents as hustling harder so you can feel worthy, laughing at jokes you don't find funny, or smiling when you want to scream.

High achievers are world-class contortionists. We learn early on how to read a room and become what's needed, and we're dang good at it. You want polished? I've got it. Chill? No problem. Assertive? Give me two seconds, I'll find the file.

I once had an Enneagram expert on my podcast. I told her that a lot of people assume I'm a 7. Without skipping a beat, she shot back, "Yeah, that's probably the version of you that you think the world wants." Oof.

It's not bad. It's adaptive. It's brilliant, actually. When you're young and trying to stay safe, being what others need you to be can protect you. It gets you the praise, the affection, the A+, the invitation. But the danger is that when you spend enough time curating versions of yourself that are lovable and acceptable, you forget who you actually are. What lights you up? What breaks your heart? What makes you feel alive? You master the performance, but you become a stranger in your own story.

And here's the tender truth. No matter how much you achieve or how many people applaud your highlight reel, you still don't feel it. You miss the love, the belonging, and the peace because, deep down, you know they're clapping for the representative, not the real you. You hear the praise, and your brain whispers, *If they only knew...*

If only they knew how hard I'm trying.
If only they knew I'm barely holding it together.
If only they knew how much of me I had to bury to be who they want.

That voice in your head isn't something to ignore. It's a warning signal. It's your inner knowing trying to get your attention. It's telling you that you're not at home to yourself. The real version of you–bold, sensitive, loud, soft, wild, ambitious–they're not too much. That version is simply unfamiliar, and you haven't given the right people a chance to love that version of you.

Here's what they don't tell you about being "high functioning:" it can feel like a prison. You're the one who has it all together. The reliable one. The competent one. The strong one. Part of you takes pride in that, but being highly functional often means being highly disconnected. You're moving fast, performing well, and getting results, but you're likely not feeling anything. Or if you are, you're pushing those feelings down to keep up the momentum.

You perform the part so well that no one thinks to ask how you're doing. And if they did, you probably wouldn't know what to say. Slowing down feels dangerous. Stillness feels suspicious. But just because you're functioning doesn't mean you're free. You can succeed on paper and feel like you're suffocating inside. That's not failure. That's feedback. That's your nervous system whispering, *We're not okay.*

The high-functioning cage comes with perks, like the color-coded planner, a well-decorated home, and Instagrammable vacations. But it also comes with bars. They're made of invisible contracts. The ones that say *I don't rest. I don't break down. I don't say no. I don't need help.*

And the cost isn't just your energy, it's your identity. Your body begins to brace on autopilot. Your shoulders tense. Your jaws tighten. Your voice becomes hesitant. Your soul grows quiet. You start forgetting what you like, what you want, and what you think. You stop checking in with yourself. You stop trusting your own yes and no. Eventually, you ghost yourself.

Friend, that's not a rough season. That's the slow erosion of self, spirit, and vitality. But it doesn't have to stay that way.

In Pursuit Insight: Performing well doesn't mean you're doing well. You can crush every goal and still feel invisible to yourself. The goal isn't to manage your image. It's to remember your essence. When you stop outsourcing your identity for approval and start reconnecting with the real you, life gets messy, but honest. And honesty is where freedom lives.

I see you. I see the part of you who craves safety and belonging. I see the part of you who wants to feel like enough and who fears being abandoned. You perform to stay ahead of judgment, to protect yourself from rejection. But here's the thing: no amount of applause can override a belief that you're not worthy. You can't out-achieve self-rejection.

And while that might sting, it's actually the best news because it means you can stop trying to earn something you already have. You can shift your focus away from how others see you and toward how you see yourself. You can write a new story about your own worth—one that doesn't need a standing ovation to be true.

Let them misunderstand you. Let them judge you. You can survive that. What you can't survive is the cost of abandoning yourself. So, let's try this. I have two questions for you. Don't overthink. Just breathe and ask:

1. What is the actual consequence of someone judging or misunderstanding you?
2. Whatever that consequence is…can you live with it?

Compass Check:
- Where in your life are you performing instead of participating?
- What part of you feels unsafe to show, and why?
- What's one small way you can practice self-loyalty this week, even if it disappoints someone else?

You don't have to become someone new. You just have to come home.

Inherited Scripts and Emotional Suppression: Trauma, Identity Confusion, and Inner Critics

You might be wondering, "What the heck is an inherited script?" Fair question. Let's start with the basics.

Inherited scripts are the unspoken rules you absorb growing up. They're the stories that tell you who you're allowed to be, how you're supposed to act, which emotions are safe to express, and which parts of yourself you should probably keep tucked away. These aren't usually delivered through a formal family meeting. No one sits you down and hands you a printed manual. They're passed on in subtler ways: a look, a scoff, a muttered comment over dinner, raised eyebrows, long silences, church sermons, coach's pep talks, locker room laughter, quiet gossip on the phone. You inhale them without realizing you're breathing them in.

These scripts come from everywhere: family, culture, religion, gender norms, class systems, geography. They sound like:

"Don't rock the boat."
"Be the good girl."
"Boys don't cry."
"Don't ask for too much."
"Stay small, stay safe."
"Ambition is selfish."
"Ambition makes your parents proud."

Do you notice the contradiction? That's part of the trap. You're told to stand out and also blend in. To be excellent and invisible. Be confident but not cocky. Be kind but not too needy. Be strong but never emotional.

I remember one summer I wanted to do something different. I wanted to work at a church camp instead of taking the usual job at Pella Windows, where I'd worked for a couple of summers to chip away at college student loans. When I told my dad, he didn't yell or forbid it. He just paused, looked at me, and said, "I'm not sure you have your priorities straight, missy."

The weight of that landed harder than any punishment.

The same thing happened when I told him I wanted to take a year off between undergrad and grad school to do full-time volunteer service for a whopping $80 a month. He couldn't wrap his head around it, and I could feel it. It was silent confusion laced with disapproval. Message received: *I don't understand you. You're making choices that don't make sense in the world I know.*

And then there was my grandma. When I told her I was becoming a life coach, she looked at me with genuine curiosity, not judgment, and said, "People will pay for that?" She wasn't trying to be mean. She was just bewildered. But again, the underlying message was clear. Value comes from doing work with your hands. It needs to be something you can see, build, and touch.

And to my brain, that translated into: *What I do isn't real. Who I am isn't right. I don't belong here.*

These messages stick because the brain's number one job is to keep you safe. And if your eight-year-old self discovered that being quiet, or helpful, or perfect earned you love or kept the peace, your brain said, "Let's do more of that." Safety locked. Approval secured. Repeat. Do it again and again, until the repetition becomes your identity. The downside is that you can't tell where the script ends and you begin.

If you're wondering why this matters, why we're digging through all this early-life rubble, it's because living by a script you didn't write will eventually break you. It doesn't happen in one big dramatic explosion. It happens in a slow, quiet erosion of self through disconnection. You'll wake up one day, stare at the life you built, and think, *Whose life is this?*

It's like wearing that itchy white sweater with the embroidered birds that your grandma gave you for Christmas when you were ten. It's not your style. It never was. But you keep wearing it because you never realized you had the option to take it off.

You're polite. You're productive. You're pleasing. You play your part beautifully. You succeed, maybe wildly, but something inside starts to stir. That still, small voice asks, *Is this really me?*

That moment right there is identity friction. It's the tug-of-war between who you became to be safe, successful, likable… and who you actually are.

And the moment that true self begins to stretch and stir, guess who shows up right on cue? Enter the Inner Critic, saluting like a good soldier: "Reporting for duty!"

This is the nervous system's self-appointed security guard. Its mission is to keep you in your lane, and more specifically, to keep you safe. It uses some of the most brutal tools. It relies on the usual suspects: shame, fear, and doubt.

It whispers:

"Who do you think you are?"
"That's not for people like us."
"You're being selfish."
"You're not ready."
"You'll embarrass yourself."
"Just be normal."
"Stay small."

You don't recognize the voice as an intruder. You think it's you. You think it's true. So you listen. You obey. You shrink. You quiet the desire. You contort yourself to fit the rules. You convince yourself that wanting more is greedy and that being yourself is risky. You believe that playing small is safer.

Before you rage against the Inner Critic and try to banish it from your mind forever, I want you to pause. This part of you isn't evil. It's not trying to ruin your life. It's trying to protect you. Poorly, yes. Inconveniently, often. But it's working with the data it collected when you were little and didn't know better. It's doing the best it can.

The real work is learning to partner with all parts of yourself, including the scared, small, doubting pieces. Invite them to sit down. Pour them tea. Ask what they're trying to say. Listen with curiosity, not contempt. Then share what you want. Reveal the dreams you're holding. Let them witness your becoming. Show them there's a new kind of safety now, one that doesn't demand self-erasure.

This is where the work gets a little spicy.

Just as your true self starts to speak and your Inner Critic raises hell, there's another layer waiting to be met. Enter emotions. The tender, messy, often inconvenient ones you've spent a lifetime trying to suppress.

This might be hard to hear, but it's true. Emotions don't disappear just because you pretend they're not there. They don't dissolve. They bury themselves in your nervous system, and they show up later in ways that don't always make sense. Irritability. Fatigue. Anxiety. Emotional flatlining. Sometimes they scream. Sometimes they sigh. Sometimes they just quietly whisper, *We're still here.*

The buildup of unprocessed emotions has a name. It's called trauma. And we need to talk about what that really means.

In Pursuit Insight:
When you feel pulled between the life you've built and the life you actually want, that tension isn't a problem. It's a messenger. Identity friction is just your soul tapping you on the shoulder, saying, *"Hey…I think we're meant for more."* *Confusion* doesn't mean you're failing. It means you're waking up.

Let's define it simply. Trauma isn't just what happened to you. It's what happened inside you as a result of what happened to you. It's what occurs when your nervous system can't metabolize an overwhelming experience. Sometimes trauma isn't loud or violent. Sometimes it's the subtle silence of your needs going unmet. It's the moment when your tears were shamed. It's the experience of having your joy feel too big for the room. It's the pain of reaching for connection and being ignored.

When you're in survival mode, you don't have time to feel. You don't have the space to process, so you suppress, and suppression becomes survival. But over time, it also becomes disconnection. Your system slams the fire doors shut, trying to contain the burn. But those doors don't just keep the fire out. They also cut off your access to the parts of you that feel, that love, that create, and long for something more.

I get it. Feeling your feelings is scary, especially when you've learned to survive without it. But here's the invitation:

Feel anyway.

Let this be your permission slip to feel what's been buried, because what's buried isn't dead. The fear, the grief, and the longing are still in there, quietly driving your decisions, your habituated patterns, and your relationships. Feeling them is how you reclaim your agency. It's how you begin to live from truth instead of protection.

This is your chance to choose healing over hiding.

Compass Check:
- What parts of your personality feel inherited rather than chosen?
- Whose voice do you hear when you doubt yourself?
- What old rules are still running the show that no longer serve your truth?
- And when you start to feel something uncomfortable, what would happen if you stayed instead of shutting down?

You get to choose the story now. You get to rewrite the script. And maybe, just maybe, the life you want isn't too much.

The Prison of the Unmanaged Mind: How Thoughts Become Cages

I like to think of the unmanaged mind like a toddler with a Sharpie in a room full of white furniture. Left unsupervised, there's a very high chance that chaos will ensue.

The brain is a thought-generating machine; that's its job. It produces upwards of 60,000 thoughts a day, and studies show that over 80% of them are negative. So, if you let it run wild without supervision, it'll default to telling stories based on faulty logic, fear, and outdated survival patterns. It's like letting a toddler run a corporation: dramatic, impulsive, severely underqualified, and entirely incapable of staying on task.

It shouts insults and contradictory commands: *You're not doing enough. You're doing too much. You're trying too hard. You're not trying hard enough. You're too much. You're not enough.*

And here's the kicker: if no one ever taught you how to think about your thoughts, you'll believe them. Not because they're true, but because they've been rehearsed so often, they feel true. That's how thoughts become cages.

So we wake up one day and wonder why everything feels so heavy. Why our goals feel hard. Why we feel tired before the work even begins. Why our once-exciting pursuits now feel like pressure cookers. It's because the brain, unchecked, spins stories rooted in fear, inadequacy, and survival. Those stories stir up anxiety, shame, dread, and doubt. And those emotions lead to self-sabotaging behaviors like procrastination, perfectionism, overworking, or avoidance, which, of course, reinforces the original story. It's a loop, and unless we interrupt it, we stay stuck.

This is what it looks like. You get an idea, a desire, or a spark of inspiration. For one moment, you feel awake. But within seconds, your mind pulls the fire alarm: *What if you fail? What will people think? Who are you to do this? You don't know how. It'll never work.* And the flood begins.

Now your body's in it. You feel tight. Your chest is heavy. Your stomach churns. Suddenly, you're overwhelmed. You tell yourself you'll start tomorrow, or you overwork to compensate, or you shrink the dream down to something "safer." And just like that, you've handed the steering wheel to a terrified toddler with a Sharpie.

You need to hear this clearly. The goal isn't to bully your brain into only thinking positive thoughts. That's spiritual bypassing dressed in self-help glitter. The goal is to understand how your mind works, learn how to partner with it, and supervise it with kindness. Your job is to guide it with curiosity and direct it with intention.

Because here's the truth. You can't out-action a belief. You can't hustle, grind, or goal-set your way out of *"I'm not good enough."* You can achieve everything you set out to do and still feel like a failure. If the story hasn't changed, the result won't matter.

And that, right there, is how thoughts become prisons—not because they're true, but because they go unchallenged. Let me show you this through the lens of a story.

The year was 2003. iPods still had click wheels, low-rise jeans were somehow socially acceptable, and a little Pixar film called *Finding Nemo* was winning hearts around the world. Do you remember Marlin? He's the neurotic clownfish who panicked his way across the Pacific in search of his son. I want to talk about Marlin because his behavior is a perfect illustration of what it looks like when the mind goes unmanaged.

Let's start by acknowledging that Marlin came by his panic honestly. A barracuda *did* take his wife and 399 fish babies. Trauma was written into his nervous system, so his brain created rules to prevent further pain: *The ocean is dangerous. Curiosity kills. Freedom is reckless.* His thoughts weren't just protective, they were commandments.

So, when Nemo expressed curiosity, Marlin panicked. He micromanaged, tried to control Nemo, and clung to his rules in a desperate attempt to ensure safety. He shrunk their world to the size of his fear. And when Nemo rebelled and swam out to touch the "butt" (yes, the boat), everything Marlin feared came true. Let's pause here.

Marlin's fear wasn't irrational, but his rules were outdated. That's what the unmanaged mind does. It takes real pain, stamps it into law, and refuses to reevaluate it. It lives in the past. It governs by fear. And in doing so, it creates a small, rigid world where risk feels lethal and control feels like love.

But then came Dory. She's the forgetful, bubbly fish who defied all of Marlin's logic. She swam toward danger. She trusted strangers. She followed instinct. She sang. And somehow, she always found a way.

At first, Marlin resisted. Her ways felt unsafe. But slowly, painfully, through laughter and loss, he began to loosen. He learned that not every unknown was dangerous. That his thoughts, while protective, weren't always right. He learned that curiosity could lead to beauty, connection, and even rescue. And (spoiler alert!) when he finally let go, he found his son. He also found *himself*.

He got access to more than the scared, rigid version of himself. He got to experience the freer, fuller one who could breathe easy again.

So yeah, it's a cartoon, but it's also a map. It's a picture of what it looks like to be run by fear, and then to choose something different. We all have a *Marlin mind*. It's trauma-coded, rule-bound, and risk-averse. It kept us safe once. But if we're not careful, it will keep us small forever.

This is where mental supervision becomes sacred. It's not about control. It's about *choice*. It's about asking:

Is this thought helping me become who I want to be?
Is this belief still true, or just familiar?
Is this fear current, or is it inherited?

Let me give you a sneak peek of the tool I'll teach you more deeply in Chapter 4, the *S.T.E.A.R. Model.*[1]

S = Situation
T = Thought
E = Emotion
A = Action
R = Result

The S.T.E.A.R. Model helps you trace your patterns. It reveals the connection between what happens around you and what you make it mean. From there, you can notice how that thought shapes your feelings, observe how those feelings drive your behavior, and recognize the results that follow.

Once you can see the loop, you gain the power to shift it.

You'll start to realize that you're not feeling anxious because of the event or "Situation." You're anxious because of the *story* you're telling yourself about the event.

That's the turning point. That's when the power shifts back into your hands. That's when you stop feeling like a prisoner of your thoughts and start showing up as an active participant in your own life.

High-functioning isn't the same as high-freedom. You can lead teams, hit numbers, speak on stages, and still live in a prison built from thoughts you aren't consciously choosing.

In Pursuit Insight:
You don't have to fix all your thoughts to be free. You just have to notice them. Name them. And choose which ones get to stay.

But you can choose now. You can pause, rethink, and rewrite.

---

[1] The concepts I share here are based on, and/or built on, tools I learned through Brooke Castillo and The Life Coach School Certification Program.

You can stop asking, *"What else do I need to do?"* and start asking, *"What do I need to believe in order to feel the way I want to feel?"*

That's the pursuit.

Compass Check:
- What's one thought you've been believing that no longer serves you?
- What might shift if you saw that thought as optional, not absolute?
- What new thought do you want to try this week?

Chapter 3:

You Are Not a Problem to Be Solved

The "Fixing" Addiction: How Self-Help Keeps Us Stuck

Here's something that the billion-dollar self-help industry doesn't exactly advertise.

Lean in so I can whisper sweet somethings in your ear: *you are not a problem to be solved.* I said what I said.

I know that might seem hard to believe when you're knee-deep in books, podcasts, coaching programs, workshops, and Pinterest-curated vision boards to help you access your highest self. That statement can feel a little... what's the word? *Sacrilegious.* I get it. I've been there too.

I've basically collected enough self-help material over the years to fill a small library branch. I've highlighted my way through Brené, underlined my way through Robbins, and covered entire chapters in sticky notes trying to *"unlock my purpose."* If you've done the same, you're certainly not alone.

Here's what I noticed, and maybe you've felt it too. Somewhere along the way, if I wasn't supervising my mind, all those growth efforts started to feel like a hustle and grind. It became another to-do list I needed to conquer to finally get *"there."*

Self-help turned into self-surveillance: *Am I being "authentic" enough? Who am I gaslighting? Who's gaslighting me? Is my mother-in-law a narcissist? Am I a narcissist?* Every "low-vibe" thought had to be reframed. Every shadow side needed to be dissected, journaled about, and turned into a breakthrough. If I wasn't actively analyzing or improving, what was I even doing?

This, my friend, is what I call the *Fixing Addiction*. It's sneaky because it looks like progress. It *feels* productive. But underneath, it's often just another disguise for unworthiness. It's another way of saying, *"I'll finally feel good enough when..."* But the goalposts always move. Remember Arrival Addiction?

The Fixing Addiction convinces you that any uncomfortable feeling is a sign of something broken. That any "stuck-ness" is evidence of failure. That unless you're constantly optimizing your life, you're somehow falling behind.

But I tend to believe the truth is way more nuanced than that.

What if the goal isn't to *feel better*, but to get better at *feeling*?

What if burnout doesn't need to be banned by adopting a new morning routine?

What if your worth doesn't need to be earned at all?

What if, stay with me here, you are not a problem to be solved, but rather something to be known?

When we view ourselves as a constant home improvement project, we risk missing the essence of who we are, what we carry, and what we came here to do. We start chasing growth so hard that we overlook the very thing we're trying to find. That includes our truth, our talents, our gifts, our voice, our perspective, and the impact only we can make. Let us not miss it.

In Pursuit Insight:
To be fully known and truly loved is one of life's greatest quests and gifts. That's kind of the whole point of this book. To be fully known requires us to stop judging ourselves and stop editing ourselves long enough so that we can actually see ourselves. Then we get to celebrate ourselves, express ourselves, and practice the skill of loving and adoring ourselves.

Here's the metaphor I like to use. I like to think of humans like vehicles. Some of us were built like Honda Civics–steady, efficient, and low maintenance. Others are more like rugged ATVs, built for bumpy roads and high-adrenaline terrain. Others are luxury vehicles, while some are load-hauling trucks. None of them is inherently better than the other. They have different functions, serve different purposes, and fulfill different needs.

We don't look at a Civic and say, "What's wrong with you that you can't off-road through a mountain trail?" We don't look at an ATV and say, "Why can't you cruise at 70 miles an hour on a paved highway with heated seats and a latte holder?"

No, we get curious about the make, the model, the features, and capacities. We learn how to take care of it and what maintenance is needed for it to run at optimal levels. We figure out what terrain it handles best. We respect the differences, and we work with the vehicle, not against it.

And yet… when it comes to ourselves, we default to *"broken"* if we're not functioning like someone else. Someone comes up with a way to optimize the workweek, and we think that's the "one right way" to do it. Someone else declares a 5 AM wake-up, cold plunge, sauna, and red-light therapy the ultimate morning routine, and we hit *add to cart* and set our alarms. We then beat ourselves up three months later when we didn't follow through and went into debt building that in-home sauna that never gets used.

But can you imagine yelling at your Civic because it's not climbing a sand dune like a Jeep Wrangler? That's what we do to ourselves when we believe the lie that we're supposed to do something different just because we aren't living, creating, hydrating, or producing the way someone else does.

You don't need to be fixed. You need to learn how you're wired. Then, you need to drive that vehicle with intention, curiosity, and care.

The tricky thing about *Fixing Addiction* is that it disguises itself as growth. It keeps you on a hamster wheel of *"not yet."* You wake up thinking, *"If I just heal this next wound…" "If I could get my morning routine perfect…" "If I could just stop having these thoughts…"*

But you're not a never-ending renovation project. You're a person. A whole, living, breathing, messy, gorgeous, multi-dimensional being.

Yes, you have edges to soften. Yes, there's room to grow. But if you don't learn the make and model of who you are, something tragic happens. You remain unknown, unexpressed, and unlived.

Don't get me wrong, self-help is powerful. But when you begin to see yourself as a problem to fix rather than a person to know, you trade connection for correction. The real issue is the compulsion, and the belief, that any version of yourself that isn't fully thriving must be a failure. It's the belief that your worthiness and wholeness depend on the next insight, the next breakthrough, the next transformation. This addiction often stems from two places:

1. Cultural Messaging:
"Be your best self!" That sounds great, until it shifts to, *"You're not enough until you're perfect."*

2. Early Wiring:
Maybe you grew up being praised for being responsible, mature, put-together, the "easy" one. So now, restlessness and messiness feel dangerous.

So instead of learning how to *be* with ourselves, we learn how to *fix* ourselves, like we're broken machines whose wires just need a quick reprogramming. But when you're constantly trying to fix yourself, you never get to meet the version of you that isn't trying to earn their right to exist. You miss out on *you*. You miss the real you who's already whole and doesn't need to prove their worth.

Listen, I'm not anti-growth. I love growing. I'm a life coach and licensed therapist, for crying out loud. I'm all for reflecting, learning, and expanding. But I also believe that growth should feel like becoming *more* of yourself, not less.

When you treat yourself like a machine that needs constant tuning, you lose touch with your humanity. Your emotions become errors. Your needs feel inconvenient. Your quirks are flaws to fix instead of signs to follow.

But when you remember you're a whole-ass person, not a self-help algorithm, you start to drive differently. You don't push your Civic to scale a mountain. You don't gaslight your ATV into cruising a six-lane freeway. You stop saying, *"What's wrong with me?"* and start asking, *"What does this version of me need right now?"*

In Pursuit Insight:
You are not a problem to be solved. You are a unique, one-of-a-kind design to be explored, known, and expressed.

That's not giving up. That's wisdom. That's building a relationship with yourself that isn't based on perfection. It's based on partnership.

And let's not forget, the odds of *you* being born–exactly you, with your particular blend of DNA, personality, timing, and soul–are estimated at 1 in 400 trillion. TRILLION, with a *T*, y'all.

That means you're not a fluke. You're a freaking **1 in 400 trillion** miracle. You are a statistical impossibility wrapped in skin. You are not a problem to be solved. You are a miracle to be witnessed, known, and expressed.

Compass Check:
- Take a breath and ask yourself, am I growing to get somewhere, or to come home to myself?
- Do I see myself as someone to fix, or someone to understand?
- What would shift if I believed nothing about me needs to be corrected to be loved?

Self-help is not the problem. The problem is the lens of constantly fixing. The problem is the belief that you are a broken, incomplete, project to perfect. But your life is not a performance review. It's a relationship. And relationships don't thrive on constant poking, prodding, and fixing. They thrive on curiosity, connection, witnessing, presence, and grace.

Yes, you can stretch. Yes, you can evolve. Please do. It's the most fun to explore every nook and cranny of who you are and what you're capable of. You just don't have to hustle your way through it. You don't have to make your goodness and wholeness contingent on figuring it all out. You already belong to yourself. You already matter. You're already enough.

And if that feels hard to believe, then you're in the right place. That's where we begin.

Inner Compass vs. Inner Critic: Build Self-Supervision, Not Self-Judgment

We've already gotten to know the Inner Critic a bit. That's the voice that desperately wants to protect us and keep us safe, albeit through misguided strategies like guilt, shame, doubt, and fear. It comes in loud and fast, dressed in alarm bells, pressure, and worst-case scenarios.

But now it's time we meet another internal character. One who has been there all along, waiting quietly beneath the noise. This is your *Inner Compass.*

Unlike the Critic, your Inner Compass doesn't shout. It doesn't panic. It doesn't demand or diminish. It offers. It invites. It speaks in the language of calm conviction, with a tone that feels like a deep exhale. This part of you knows. It leads with clarity and wisdom, not control and worry.

The tricky part is that their voices can get tangled, especially if you've spent your life wired for performance, hypervigilance, or survival. One of the most powerful practices I've found for untangling them, and getting to know them better, is to give these parts full character sketches, like casting roles in a movie. When you see them clearly, you get to decide who holds the microphone.

I call my Inner Critic "Negative Nancy." She wears a tight blue pencil skirt and an equally tight white blouse, cinched with a thick red belt. Her matching red reading glasses teeter at the edge of her nose. Her bun is too high. Her clipboard is always clutched at her chest. And she keeps a pencil in hand, either tapping with judgment or scribbling furiously, noting everything I'm supposedly doing wrong. Nancy is loud, rigid, and relentless. She is the voice of pressure and panic, and she often arrives before I even realize I've invited her in.

My Inner Compass? Well, she needs two characters. Don't ask me why, I've accepted it.

One is Glinda the Good Witch. She is graceful, glowing, and calm. The other is The Magician from the tarot deck, a mysterious and grounded figure who bridges the spirit world and the material world, fully sovereign and wise. Maybe my unconscious mind knows it takes a duo to counter Nancy's volume. Or maybe it's just my brain's way of stacking the deck. Either way, these are my guides.

The Inner Compass speaks with curiosity, compassion, clarity, and courage. Her voice is a whisper that asks me to get still, to go inward, to spelunk through the layers of noise and fear until I find her truth.

When she speaks, it's not performative, it's peaceful. She doesn't scold. She invites.

This is the heart of self-supervision. This isn't the same as self-judgment, perfecting, or controlling. This is supervision and guidance, the kind that says: *"I see you. I'll listen. I'll choose from alignment, not anxiety."*

I like to think of the mind as a meeting room. Around the table sits your entire internal cast; the Dreamer, the Strategist, the Skeptic, the Inner Child, Fear, the Critic, the Protector, and maybe even more.

The key is simple. They all have voices, but none of them is the CEO. You are. And your Inner Compass serves as your lead advisor. This doesn't mean silencing any parts. It's quite the opposite, actually.

Everyone gets a seat. Everyone gets to speak. But not everyone gets to lead. You listen. You acknowledge. And then, you make a conscious choice about how to move forward. It's how you honor all of you without being ruled by any one piece.

This is how you shift from a fear-based pursuit to a purpose-based pursuit.

Compassionate Interception: A Four-Step Practice

When the Inner Critic takes hold, it can feel impossible to break free from the spiral of self-judgment and fear. Here's a practical tool to help you interrupt that pattern and reconnect with your authentic guidance: *Compassionate Interception.*

This four-step process creates space between you and your critical thoughts, allowing you to access your deeper wisdom and make choices from a place of truth rather than fear.

Step 1: Notice

The first step is recognizing when your Inner Critic has arrived. You'll know them by their signature calling cards: urgency, pressure, comparison, panic, or perfectionism. Listen for the language they use, red flag thoughts often include *"should," "always,"* and *"never."*

The moment you catch yourself in that familiar spiral, you've already taken the most important step. Awareness is the beginning of choice.

Step 2: Name It

Don't let the critical voice operate in the shadows. Call it out directly. Write it down, say it out loud, or simply acknowledge it internally: *"Ah, this is Negative Nancy. She's trying to keep me safe with shame. I hear her. But this isn't the whole truth."*

Naming the voice strips it of some of its power and creates distance between you and the criticism. You are not your thoughts, you are the observer of them.

Step 3: Pause and Ask

After acknowledging the Critic, create a moment of stillness. Take a breath and ask: *"What does my Inner Compass have to say?"*

Get quiet. Even thirty seconds of presence can shift your entire frequency from reactive to receptive. This pause is where the magic happens. It's the space where your truest guidance can emerge.

If you're having trouble accessing your Inner Compass, try this visualization exercise, adapted from Melissa Tiers, founder of The Center for Integrative Hypnosis:

The Staircase to Your Inner Compass

1. Imagine yourself standing at the top of a beautiful staircase. You'll count backward from 10 to 1, stepping down with each number.

2. At the bottom waits a beautiful doorway. On the other side, your Inner Compass.

3. Close your eyes. Take a deep breath. Feel your body supported by your seat or the ground.

4. Begin your descent:

   - **10:** Exhale and take one step down
   - **9:** Feel yourself relaxing deeper
   - **8:** Drop inward, toward your inner self
   - **7:** Each step down softens you more
   - **6:** Releasing tension with every breath
   - **5:** Halfway down, feeling more connected
   - **4:** Deeper into your inner wisdom
   - **3:** Almost there, trusting the process
   - **2:** One more step toward your truth
   - **1:** You've arrived

5. At the bottom, approach the door and open it.

6. Notice your Inner Compass. How do they stand? What are they wearing? What's their energy like?

7. Ask whatever you need to know. Trust what arises, even if it doesn't immediately "make sense."

Step 4: Choose on Purpose
Based on what your Inner Compass reveals, make your next move. This choice might not be the easiest path. It might be inconvenient or uncomfortable, but it will be authentic, and that's what matters.

Your Inner Compass speaks in the language of truth, not convenience. Trust what emerges, even when it challenges your assumptions or comfort zone.

Remember, this is practice, not performance. If you find yourself still following the Critic or acting from fear after using this process, that's completely normal. This isn't about perfect execution, it's about building a new relationship with your inner experience.

In Pursuit Insight:
Your Inner Critic is trying to protect you from pain. Your Inner Compass is trying to lead you toward the truth. Only one of them knows who you really are.

Each time you practice Compassionate Interception, you're strengthening your ability to choose consciousness over reactivity. You're training yourself to pause, listen, and respond from your deepest wisdom rather than your loudest fears.

Be patient with yourself as you develop this skill. Like any practice, it gets stronger with repetition and gentler with self-compassion.

Compass Check:
- Is this thought rooted in fear or freedom?
- Am I shrinking or expanding right now?
- Who am I trying to please or protect?
- If I trusted myself completely, what would I do next?

Write these questions down. Save them in your phone. Tattoo them on your wrist if you want. (Kidding. Kind of.)

Freedom doesn't mean you never hear the Critic again. It means you don't automatically obey. It means you can stay present in the tension long enough to choose truth over fear. That's alignment. That's liberation. That's the pursuit.

Becoming Your Own Safe Place: Reparenting the Self With Compassion

Can we all agree on one thing? Or maybe just agree to disagree? You are human—a beautifully complex being with real emotional needs that, maybe, just maybe, weren't met the way you needed them to be.

If you're anything like the people I coach (myself included), you probably learned early on that it wasn't safe to show too much, need too much, or feel too much. So, you armored up. You took care of everyone else. You became high-functioning as hell. And slowly, almost without noticing, you stopped checking in on the one person who needed you most: yourself.

If no one's ever asked you this before, I will. Who's been taking care of you?

For many of us, the honest answer is no one. We weren't taught how to care for ourselves emotionally. We learned how to hustle, cope, and perform, but not how to connect or self-soothe. We weren't shown how to lead ourselves with gentleness and grace. And we certainly were not taught how to make ourselves feel safe when the world feels like too much.

That's where the concept of reparenting comes in. This isn't just a trendy buzzword. It's a revolutionary act of self-leadership.

Reparenting is the practice of becoming the grounded, loving, emotionally attuned adult you didn't always have growing up. It's about meeting yourself now with the same tenderness, wisdom, and care that you needed then. Not because your parents were terrible (though maybe they were), but because most people are operating with an outdated emotional toolkit and passing down the best they've got.

This isn't about blame. It's about ownership, responsibility, and reclaiming power. It's time to take back the reins. Reparenting means I don't need to keep repeating the emotional patterns I inherited. I can write a new story. I can build a new kind of safety inside myself, for myself, and from myself.

You need this safety. Without it, you'll keep outsourcing your sense of worth. You'll keep hustling for validation. You'll keep abandoning your truth to keep the peace. And you'll wonder why you're exhausted and resentful even though you've "done everything right."

We all need an emotional home–a place where it's safe to fall apart, to be seen, and to feel all the things without being told we're too much or not enough. If that home didn't exist around you growing up, then it's time to build one within you. That's what reparenting is. It's the sacred work of saying to yourself, *"I've got you now."*

This begins with recognizing the parts of you that need your care the most. Think about your inner child, not in some cheesy, woo-woo way, but for real. There's a version of you who still panics when someone's angry, still feels the sting of rejection, still wants to run and hide when you mess up. That part isn't irrational, it's simply unhealed.

It's the part that was told, directly or indirectly, that certain emotions weren't welcome, that mistakes made you unlovable, that your needs were too much. That part of you doesn't need fixing, it needs *you*.

I used to carry a lot of shame for not having people show up for me. I didn't have parents or family members at my softball games, basketball games, or drill team performances. I remember scanning the crowd, hoping maybe this time someone would be there for me. Maybe someone would think I was worth showing up for.

As an adult, I've come to understand something important. Even if the people who were "supposed to" show up for me throughout life didn't, there was one person who always did: *me*. I kept showing up. As a kid, it felt like survival, but now I recognize it as my inner advocate. There was a part of me who was always watching out for me, standing in for me, and refusing to give up on me. Today, I get to show up for myself on purpose and from love.

I got curious about what the younger me might need, so I tried a little guided imagery to see if she had anything to say. She looked to be about six years old. When I asked her what she needed, she didn't ask for a pep talk or a plan. She asked me to hold her hand and go roller skating with her. So I did. I pictured us at the rink, shaky at first, giggling by the arcade, two versions of me moving in rhythm, having a blast.

These days, I keep a photo in my desk drawer. It's a snapshot of my cute-as-hell four-year-old self with a photoshopped picture of my adult self right beside her. The caption reads, *"That's my girl. I've got your back. Always."* This kind of activity might feel mushy, awkward, or even a little cringey. I get it, and do it anyway. This kind of loving attention heals something deep and essential. I promise.

Reparenting is how you rebuild trust with that part of yourself. And yes, it's awkward at first. It won't feel natural because most of us were never taught how to be with ourselves this way. But it *is* possible, and it's where healing actually begins.

Dr. Dan Siegel talks about the "4 Ss" that help children develop secure attachment. He explains that they need to feel safe, seen, soothed, and secure. These aren't just childhood needs, they are *human* needs. If you didn't get them then, you're likely still craving them now. The good news is, you can start giving them to yourself, right now.

In Pursuit Insight:
You don't have to wait for someone else to choose you, see you, love you, or save you. You are allowed to be the one who does that for yourself. It may not be fair. But you deserve it anyway.

Safety means creating an internal and external environment where you feel protected. It's saying no without guilt. It's canceling the plan when your soul is tired. It's deciding not to bulldoze past your limits just to keep up appearances. Safety sounds like, *"I won't ditch myself to make other people comfortable."* It's the fierce decision to have your own back, no matter what.

Being seen means acknowledging your own experience with compassion instead of judgment. You stop brushing things off with, *"I shouldn't feel this way."* Instead, it's, *"Yep. That hit hard. Of course I feel something."* It's giving yourself a front-row seat to your own experience, messy mascara tears and all. When you allow yourself to be fully seen, first by you, you stop needing to perform for belonging.

Soothing is when you become the calm in your own storm. It's the practice of regulating your nervous system when it feels overwhelmed. And no, it doesn't require a silent retreat or a stack of self-help books (unless that's your thing). Sometimes, it's as simple as taking a deep breath and whispering, *"We're okay. I'm here."* It's speaking to yourself like a wise, steady best friend. It's stepping out of the shame spiral and choosing compassion over criticism.

Security begins to build when the first three S's are practiced consistently. It takes root when this becomes a way of life, not a one-time self-care checklist. When you practice safety, visibility, and soothing on repeat, something wild happens. You begin to trust yourself. You stop abandoning yourself the moment life gets hard. You become someone you can count on.

That's not just growth. That's coming home.

You don't have to overhaul your life overnight. Start with micro-moments. When you mess up, catch yourself before the Inner Critic takes over and say, *"It's okay. I'm learning."* When you're overwhelmed, put a hand on your chest and ask, *"What do I need right now?"* Then actually listen.

These tiny choices compound over time. They retrain your nervous system, build internal safety, and bring you home to yourself. The strongest, wisest, most powerful version of you doesn't come from hustle or hyper-independence. It's born from love. It comes from choosing to stop abandoning yourself and learning to stand by your own side, especially when life gets hard.

You don't need another productivity hack. You don't need another title or external win. You need a relationship with yourself that feels like a soft place to land. That's the foundation for everything else.

Let me say this clearly, with all the love I can muster. If no one ever taught you how to do this, it's not your fault. Truly. But it *is* your responsibility now. You have the power to lead yourself in a new way. You get to turn your inner world into a place you actually want to live.

You don't have to perfect it, you just have to make peace with it. You're not weak for needing emotional safety. You're wise for learning how to create it.

Compass Check:
- Pause and ask yourself: What did I need, or need to hear, as a kid that I can give or say to myself today?

Write it down. Repeat it daily. Let it become your new baseline.

The real magic of reparenting is that it teaches you how to lead yourself with compassion, clarity, and grounded self-trust. And that's everything in a world that's constantly trying to distract, define, and derail you.

This might be a hard truth to hear, but it's important: no one else can do this work for you. A partner cannot do it. A coach cannot do it. A therapist cannot do it. A title, paycheck, or accomplishment will not do it. Only you can build the kind of relationship with yourself where it feels safe to be all of who you are. That includes the messy, tender, and vulnerable parts.

You don't have to earn that safety. You just have to choose it. And when you do, that's when the magic happens. You stop performing and start becoming. You stop striving and start listening. You stop chasing and start receiving. You start living like someone who belongs to yourself, to your truth, and to your own dang life.

My invitation to you is this: don't cement yourself in the "prison." I get it. Setbacks, shame, and detours can start to feel like a life sentence. But just because it happened doesn't mean it has to define you. It's part of your story, it's not the whole story.

As Nelson Mandela once said, *"As I walked out the door toward the gate that would lead to my freedom, I knew if I didn't leave my bitterness and hatred behind, I'd still be in prison."*

Take a moment to reflect on that quote. How often do we drag our old stories into our new seasons? We carry our regrets, mistakes, and survival strategies. Sometimes we carry them like badges of honor, proof of who we were. Other times we drag them like 100-pound weights, heavy with limiting beliefs about who we were and who we're allowed to become.

But you're not who you used to be. Don't miss who you are now because you're too focused on who you were.

I recently met an 80-year-old woman who was fit, vibrant, and full of life. I approached her because I was dying to know her secret to living a full life. Here's what she said to me: *"I never shied away from a good reinvention."*

That line stuck with me. Reinvention isn't about becoming someone different. It's about coming home to yourself again and again. It's about choosing to evolve and to live forward. That's the work. That's the invitation.

Whether it's addiction, burnout, grief, or the chaos of an unmanaged mind, I've walked with people through it all. I've walked it myself. At this point, I'm basically a walking locksmith. I help people open what's been closed. Yes, doors can slam shut. Sometimes they lock tight, but that's never the end. With the right tools and the right mindset, there's always a way forward.

Let's get you on the path.

PART II:

THE PATH

Living the Freedom Formula

Chapter 4:

SEE the Blocks

Spot the Pattern: How Beliefs Run the Show

Ally's Story

Ally closes her laptop at 11:47 p.m., again. The pitch deck is finally finished, even though it's not due until next week. Her eyes are burning. Her thoughts are fuzzy. She skipped dinner again.

She promises herself she'll rest tomorrow. She always says that, but resting without "earning" it makes her skin crawl, like she's broken some internal law. Her body's begging her to stop, but her mind is whispering a deeper warning:

"If you slow down, you'll lose your edge."

That voice sounds a lot like survival–like the quiet panic of never being enough unless you're achieving something.

Ally isn't lazy. She isn't addicted to stress because she loves the rush. She's not a productivity junkie because hustle culture is just so inspiring. She's on autopilot. She's being steered by an internalized belief that got installed before she even knew she was allowed to question it:

"Your worth is what you produce."

Her nervous system doesn't recognize slowness as peace. It registers it as a threat. If you saw yourself in Ally, even just a little, keep reading. This is for you.

You Cannot Change What You Cannot See

No matter how ambitious you are, how many affirmations you repeat, or how vividly you've mapped out your Future Self, none of it will matter if you don't see the conscious and unconscious beliefs running the show. Those beliefs will keep driving your life on autopilot.

This is a problem because that autopilot setting probably wasn't even programmed by you, at least not entirely, and usually not consciously.

See, your brain is a loyal, pattern-loving, meaning-associating, shortcut-seeking little machine. It doesn't care about your soul's fulfillment, your calling, or your therapist's notes about secure attachment. It cares about efficiency and survival.

It's not wired to make you feel amazing. It's wired to keep you alive using the most energy-conserving methods possible, and from that perspective, your brain has been absolutely crushing it.

Are you thriving? Living in alignment? Breaking generational patterns and becoming the freest version of yourself? That requires a different kind of attention.

If you've ever wondered why you keep circling the same block in life, why you land in the same relationship dynamics, the same financial ruts, the same burnout cycles, despite all your personal growth, self-awareness, and good intentions... welcome to the Pattern Club. We all have a membership card.

These unconscious patterns didn't just show up overnight. Most of them were installed when you were young, sponge-brained, and highly susceptible. You absorbed them from the people, environments, and systems that shaped your early worldview. They embedded beliefs in your nervous system long before you had the developmental skillset to question, reject, or replace them.

Think of it like this. Your mind was a blank screen, and someone handed you a software package, one filled with beliefs about love, worth, safety, success, truth, and power. You clicked "accept all" without reading the terms and conditions because, well, you didn't even know there were terms.

Now, as an adult, you're walking around trying to build an aligned life on outdated software that keeps glitching every time you try to rest, speak up, or dream bigger. Let me show you what that looks like in real life.

Identify the Belief

What's really driving the burnout loop? For Ally, it might sound like:

- *"I am only valuable if I'm producing something."*
- *"Slowing down is dangerous."*

The work isn't just about forcing yourself to shut the laptop earlier. It starts deeper than that. It starts with asking:

- Is this belief true?
- Where did it come from?
- Is it even mine?
- Is it serving me?
- If not, what would a better belief sound like?

Let's look at another example.

Deja's Story

Deja agrees to chair another committee. It wasn't part of her plan. She had intentionally blocked that weekend for rest, writing, maybe even some long-overdue dreaming. But when the request came in, her first instinct to say no was quickly steamrolled by guilt. The weight of potential disapproval, even if only imagined, felt unbearable.

So instead of honoring her truth, she offered a small, well-meaning lie. It wasn't out of malice. It was just enough to keep the peace. She put on her well-practiced smile and said, *"Happy to help!"* while a quiet ache bloomed in her chest. Her calendar is full. Her spirit is not.

Deja's childhood taught her that love was a reward for compliance, not a right. She came to believe that, in order to feel safe, she had to be agreeable. To gain acceptance, she had to make herself constantly available. And in order to belong, she had to betray her own needs and abandon herself.

From the outside, Deja looks like she's winning. She's polished, capable, and dependable. But on the inside, she's exhausted from managing the performance. What she thought would bring her fulfillment has only deepened the hollowness.

Maybe your inner Deja has been in the driver's seat too.

Her unconscious scripts might sound like:

- *"My needs are less important than other people's comfort."*
- *"Love is conditional."*

Ask yourself: What beliefs are guiding your yeses? Are they rooted in alignment or fear of disappointing someone?

Maya's Story

Then there's Maya. She lights up when she talks about her dream to write a book, start a podcast, or create something that feels fully hers. She longs to do something that is creatively, spiritually, and soulfully aligned. However, when she opens the laptop to begin, all she hears is silence. Then the doubt creeps in.

- *"What's the point?"*
- *"Other people are already doing this, and better."*
- *"I'm not ready. I don't know enough."*

So, she closes the screen again. The desire is still there, and it's not a lack of ability holding her back. What's holding her back is that she is unconsciously filtering her dream through the belief that she has to be flawless to begin. She's afraid that being seen means being vulnerable and that vulnerability equals risk.

If you felt a pang reading that, here's what might be underneath:

- *"I have to know how it all works before I begin."*
- *"If I'm not the best, I shouldn't try."*
- *"My voice only matters once I've earned it."*

The size of your dream isn't what's holding you back. It's the beliefs wrapped around your readiness, your worthiness, and your capability. The good news is that those beliefs can be reprogrammed once you're willing to *see* them.

Compass Check:
- What's one recurring pattern or behavior in your life that doesn't feel aligned but keeps showing up?
- What belief might be quietly fueling that behavior?

Now pause, *really* pause. How many of your beliefs about love, rest, success, identity, or worth did you actually choose as an adult? I'm not talking about the beliefs that feel familiar or the ones that got applause. I'm talking about the ones you consciously adopted as truth because they aligned with your values.

Probably not many.

Most of us are still living according to inherited rubrics. Things like:

"Be the perfect parent or you'll ruin your kids."
"Don't shine too bright."
"Work hard. Don't complain."
"Rest is weakness."
"Be liked. Not honest."

In Pursuit Insight:
You can't change what's unconsciously running the show. But when you spot the belief behind the pattern, you shift from reacting to becoming aware. And awareness is the birthplace of freedom.

If these go unchecked, they become default settings, and default settings have authority. They steer our lives without consent. Sometimes, without even our awareness.

There's a story about how elephants are trained. When they're small, they're tied to a thick rope anchored deep in the ground. They pull and tug, try to break free, but they're not strong enough. Eventually, they stop trying. Years later, when they're massive and powerful, easily capable of snapping the rope with one movement, they stay put. It is the same flimsy rope. A belief installed long ago keeps them from testing their strength. They don't pull anymore. It's not because they can't, but because they believe they can't.

Does that sound familiar?

At some point, someone handed you a limit and told you it was your truth. That's the rope.

When you say, *"Oh, I'm a perfectionist. I'm a people-pleaser,"* that's not exactly accurate. You might engage in perfectionist behavior or people-pleasing behavior, but it's not your identity. It isn't a fixed trait. It's not who you are. It's just programming, and luckily, programming can be rewritten.

Let's break it down:

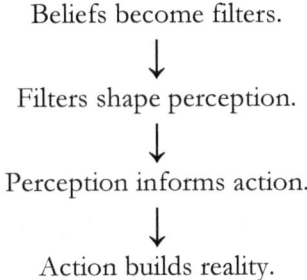

Beliefs become filters.

↓

Filters shape perception.

↓

Perception informs action.

↓

Action builds reality.

If you believe you're not enough, your brain filters the world looking for evidence. Your mind skips over the praise but clings to the one sideways comment. You dismiss compliments and obsess over criticism. This isn't because they're truer, it's because they match the filter. The lens gets foggy, and you live inside the story the fog tells.

Let's say your mental filter is, "*I always mess things up.*" You're in a team meeting, and your idea doesn't land. Immediately, your inner narrator says, "*See? I knew it. I'm not cut out for this.*" You shrink. You hesitate next time. You pull back.

Now imagine someone else in the same meeting, in that same moment. Their thought might be, "*Okay, that didn't land yet. I'll tweak it and try again.*" One moment, two different realities. The only difference is the lens each person is using. Changing your life begins by changing your lens, and that starts with spotting the pattern.

You don't have to shame yourself for your patterns. You just have to notice them with curiosity and compassion. "Oh hey, look at that. I say yes when I want to say no. I fix things that aren't mine. I don't celebrate wins because I'm afraid it'll all fall apart."
Noticing = power. Denying = stuck.

Start by tuning in to your inner narrator. That voice isn't always wise. Sometimes it's a scared 12-year-old. Sometimes it's your dad's criticism. Sometimes it's a toxic theology, or a wounded teacher, or a former boss. You get to say, "*Thanks for your input. I'm choosing differently now.*"

This is not about blaming. This is about reclaiming. You don't have to drag your childhood into every adult decision, but you do have to admit that your patterns didn't come from nowhere.

As Jung said, *"Until you make the unconscious conscious, it will direct your life, and you will call it fate."*

So, call it what it is. It's programming. It's not personality or destiny. It is a set of unconscious codes that have been running the show. The good news is, you are the one holding the keyboard now. That means you have the power to rewrite the program.

Freedom Starts with Awareness: Using the S.T.E.A.R. Model to Navigate Anxiety, Decision-Making, and Pursuit

If you're anything like me, you've read all the books. You've gone down the rabbit hole of YouTube videos. You've followed the experts, filled out the planners, and tried the templates. You've applied the five-step strategies for launching the business, falling in love, losing the weight, growing the bank account, or finally breaking your social media addiction. You know how to chase a goal.

But if you don't know what's really driving your current behavior, or how to intentionally drive a new one, then nothing sticks. You just end up rehearsing the same loop in a different costume.

This is where I teach you what I half-jokingly call the secrets of the universe. I don't call them that because they're mystical or hard to grasp. I call them that because once you truly get this, everything changes.

You have to become deeply honest about what you're thinking. It might feel uncomfortable at times, but it is always liberating. You must get curious about the thoughts driving your actions, especially the ones hiding beneath the surface of your stress, your stuck-ness, and your self-sabotage. Because the truth is, you cannot change what you are unwilling or unable to see.

Action without awareness is just another performance, and you've done that dance before. But if you're here, if you're still reading, then I don't think you're chasing more hacks. You're chasing something deeper.

You're not after more productivity; you're after peace. You're not just here to build a life that looks good. You want one that feels good too. And that kind of life starts with seeing your mind clearly.

Most people have no idea how to do this. Not because they're broken, lazy, or incapable, but because they were never shown how.

We're trained to scan the world outside of us. We analyze every comment, every missed opportunity, and every productivity hack. We obsess over what they meant, why we didn't get the promotion, or which morning routine made that billionaire successful.

Turning that same level of attention inward, toward your own thoughts, habits, and emotional reflexes, is possible. It's a skill. It's something you can learn. And I'm going to teach you how.

There are two simple tools I use every day, both personally and with clients, that help build this muscle of awareness. These tools are the *Thought Download* and the *S.T.E.A.R. Model*.[2] They'll teach you to see your brain without judgment, so you can lead your life with intention.

The Thought Download
Let's start with the simplest and most revealing practice, the Thought Download.

This is not journaling for the sake of journaling. This isn't a "Dear Diary" from fifth grade about your crush or a bullet-point recap of today's to-do list. This is a raw, unfiltered brain dump. It's a moment of radical honesty, like eavesdropping on your thoughts as if they belonged to someone else.

Set a timer. Five minutes works well, but two or ten is fine too. Then start writing. No editing. No censoring. No pretending. Don't write what you *should* be thinking. Don't write what you *wish* you believed. Write what's real, what's raw, and what's running the show behind the scenes.

This is you turning the lights on in a messy closet and choosing curiosity instead of shame.

Your thoughts don't have to be profound to be powerful. You might jot down things like:

---

2 The concepts I share here are based on, and/or built on, tools I learned through Brooke Castillo and The Life Coach School Certification Program.

"I feel behind."
"I'm annoyed with my partner."
"No one sees how hard I'm trying."
"I'm not good at sticking with things."

Boom. That right there is gold. That's your material. That's the internal operating system you've been running, whether you realized it or not.

Before you can rewire anything, you have to see it. This isn't about fixing your thoughts. It's about observing them.

You cannot interrupt a belief you've never named. You can't shift a narrative you haven't brought into awareness. And you definitely can't change a pattern you are unwilling to look at.

Here are a few prompts to get you started:

- What thoughts are getting in my way?
- I notice my brain is telling me...
- What am I thinking right now?
- Where am I compared to where I want to be?
- Why is this a problem?

Once the timer dings and your brain dump is complete, it's time to go deeper.

The S.T.E.A.R. Model: A Framework for Self-Awareness

This is the single most powerful model I know for helping people understand what's driving their feelings, actions, and results. It's where psychology meets practicality, and it's changed my life.

S.T.E.A.R. stands for:

- Situation
- Thought
- Emotion
- Action
- Result

Let's break it down.

Situation: This is the part of reality that's factual. No adjectives. No interpretation. No "always" or "never" or "so rude." Just the neutral, factual, data.

Example: *"My boss emailed me at 7 p.m. asking for a report."*
That's a neutral situation. It's observable. Verifiable. No drama.

Compare that to *"My boss is so overbearing and has no respect for boundaries."*
That's not a Situation. That's a Thought.

Thought: This is what you *make* the situation mean. It's the sentence in your mind. It's not the truth, it's an interpretation. This is where you reclaim your power, because even if you didn't choose the thought originally, you can choose to question it now.

Examples of thoughts in response to that 7 p.m. email:

"She doesn't respect my time."
"I'm expected to be available 24/7."
"If I don't respond, I'll seem lazy."

All thoughts are optional. They may feel automatic, but that doesn't mean they're true or useful.

Emotion: This is the feeling that arises from the thought. One word. Not a sentence. If you say, "I feel like I'm drowning," that's a metaphor, not a feeling. We're looking for words such as anxious, frustrated, sad, empowered, ashamed, hopeful.

"She doesn't respect my time" might create resentment.
"I can never log off" might generate pressure or helplessness.

For the purposes of The S.T.E.A.R. Model, I use the terms "feelings" and "emotions" interchangeably.

Action: This is what you do, or avoid doing, because of that emotion. Most people try to change their actions first, but without examining the thought that caused the emotion, behavior change won't stick. Trying to change the action without changing the thought and emotion fueling it will result in surface-level and/or time-limited change at best.

When you're identifying the actions coming from the thought and emotion combo in the Model you're working on, you want to list all your actions, inactions, reactions, coping mechanisms, and mental habits. The more you put in the Action line, the better you will be able to see the Result you create with this particular thought and emotion combination.

Here are some example actions from frustration. You say yes even though you want to say no. You stew. You complain to a friend. You procrastinate. You spiral. You blame. You don't set boundaries and work late. You judge (yourself and others involved in the Situation). You avoid the real conversation you need to have.

Result: This is the outcome you create from your actions and inactions. It's the punchline of the Model. It's the mirror that reflects your original thought right back at you.

Let's walk it through:
- **S**: Boss emailed at 7 p.m. asking for a report
- **T**: She doesn't respect my time
- **E**: Frustration
- **A**: I say yes (even though I don't want to). I work on the report after hours. I stay up late ruminating on why my boss is wrong. I judge my boss. I look for evidence to support the thought that she doesn't respect me. I don't set boundaries. I don't think about or prioritize what I need.
- **R**: I don't respect my own time

See how that works? A thought like "She doesn't respect my time" doesn't just sit in your mind, it becomes the lens through which you interpret everything. You tense up when she speaks, your tone gets sharp, you withdraw or over-explain, and suddenly, you've shown up in ways that reinforce the very thing you feared. That thought becomes a self-fulfilling prophecy.

This is where the S.T.E.A.R. Model becomes such a powerful tool. It's not about forcing your mind to think happy thoughts or slapping positivity over real issues. It's about becoming a conscious observer of your mind so you can interrupt the loop.

The truth is, most of us are running models we didn't consciously choose. We inherited beliefs from childhood, religion, trauma, family dynamics, or cultural messaging. These mental-emotional loops become default operating systems. And because they feel familiar, we assume they're true. But familiarity doesn't equal truth.

When you start seeing your model and are able to name the thought that's driving your emotion, your action, and your result, you take the first step toward reclaiming your agency. That's not surface-level mindset work. That's deep, liberating, life-altering awareness.

The S.T.E.A.R. Model helps you map the invisible chain reaction from thought to outcome. Most of us never slow down enough to ask: *"What's actually driving this behavior? What's the story I'm believing right now?"*

Here's a fun fact you might not know. Of the five components in the S.T.E.A.R. Model (Situation, Thought, Emotion, Action, Result), only one is outside your control: the **Situation**. You don't control your boss's tone in an email, your partner's facial expression, or the traffic jam. But you do control how you interpret what's happening. That interpretation, also known as the thought, is the real power player. It determines how you feel, how you respond, how you behave, and ultimately, what result you create.

And here's where it gets really exciting. Once you can name the thought, you can choose to think something different.

That is power.
That is agency.
That is freedom.

The S.T.E.A.R. Model isn't just a tool for clarity; it's a tool for choice. It reveals why you feel stuck, why you keep reacting in certain ways, and how your inner world is shaping your external results. Once you see it, you can start to shift it.

Most people are walking around living in what I call *unintentional models*. These are driven by old wiring, habitual thoughts, and stories that were never examined, just repeated. These models feel like "just the way it is," when in reality, they're just highly practiced ways of thinking.

But you don't have to keep rehearsing the same old script.

Once you start identifying unintentional models, you can begin creating *intentional* ones. You choose thoughts on purpose, thoughts that feel believable, that generate aligned emotions, and lead to grounded actions with meaningful results.

This isn't the kind of work that involves denial or spiritual bypassing. This is about creating change from sovereignty.

It begins with the truth that you are not at the mercy of your thoughts.

You are the thinker.
You get to be the author.
You get to decide the story you're living from.

Let's look at a few real-world examples:

Anxiety Example

Component	Unintentional	Intentional
Situation (S)	I have a presentation tomorrow.	I have a presentation tomorrow.
Thought (T)	I'm going to mess this up.	I can be both prepared and human.
Emotion (E)	Anxiety	Grounded or confident
Action (A)	I procrastinate preparing, over-rehearse in my head, stay up late spiraling, think about what I don't know, worry about what people will think of me, avoid eye contact with audience, fumble over words.	Schedule a time to prepare, review the material, practice once or twice, go to bed at a reasonable hour, and remind myself it's okay to feel a little nervous, don't ruminate about what ifs, focus on what I can control, don't spend time on what I can't control, present with presence.
Result (R)	I show up sleep-deprived and underprepared, reinforcing the belief that I'm not good at this.	I show up well-rested, connected to my message, deliver a presentation I feel good about.

Relationship Example

Component	Unintentional	Intentional
Situation (S)	My partner asked, *"Are you going out again tonight?"*	My partner asked, *"Are you going out again tonight?"*
Thought (T)	They're trying to control me.	I wonder why they're asking that.
Emotion (E)	Defensive	Curiosity
Action (A)	I snap back, say things I wish I hadn't, walk out, don't respond to texts, don't get curious, don't ask questions, don't check in with how I feel or communicate it.	Pay attention to the stories my brain offered in response to their question, share the story I'm telling myself, ask questions, seek clarification, share my plans, don't shut down or walk away.
Result (R)	I don't create the connection and understanding I desire in the relationship (aka, I don't control how I show up).	I create connection and understanding with myself and my partner.

Goal Example

Component	Unintentional	Intentional
Situation (S)	Goal to launch my business	Goal to launch my business
Thought (T)	I'm not ready.	I don't have to be perfect to start.
Emotion (E)	Doubt	Courage
Action (A)	I stall, take another course, tweak the logo for the 47th time, don't tell anyone about my business, don't make offers, think about what could go wrong, focus on what I don't know, don't think about what could go right or how much value the business could offer.	I choose a first offer and launch it to a small audience, track my progress, remind myself that feedback is data, not failure.
Result (R)	My business stays an idea in my head, not a reality.	I start a business (create momentum, get my idea into the world, and learn what works, proving I can move forward imperfectly.)

Decision-Making Example

Component	Unintentional	Intentional
Situation (S)	I was offered a new job in a different city.	I was offered a new job in a different city.
Thought (T)	There's so much at stake.	There isn't one "right" answer.
Emotion (E)	Overwhelm	Open
Action (A)	I ruminate, poll 13 friends, spiral, delay making a decision, don't think about what I want, think about the risks of saying yes, think about the risks of saying no, don't focus on possibilities, don't think about how to make either option right for me.	Pause, write out pros/cons, reflect on what matters most, consider short-term and long-term risks/benefits, map out how I could make either decision right for me.
Result (R)	I miss out on pursuing what I want.	I create a win-win for myself.

This kind of awareness is a total superpower. Not in a flashy, control-the-universe kind of way, but in a grounded, life-changing, freedom-giving kind of way. When you learn to see yourself clearly through the gentle lens of curiosity instead of the harsh lens of judgment, you unlock real power. You access the kind of power that lets you spot self-sabotaging patterns without spiraling. It allows you to pause before reacting and gives you space to ask, *"Is this thought actually true?"* and *"Is it serving me?"* When the answer is no, you get to choose again.

You can un-believe the unhelpful thoughts. You can practice building belief in ones that feel a little better, or at least less terrible, and a lot more useful. You start to notice the parts of you that get activated and meet them with compassion instead of shame. That creates space. And in that space, you evolve. You grow. You heal. You begin to respond from alignment instead of reacting from fear or defense.

This is how you become someone who doesn't have to control everything around you just to feel safe. That becomes available to you because you've learned to create safety within yourself. And if I'm honest, I think that's a big freaking deal.

This is why awareness isn't just the first step, it's woven into the entire process. It's what allows you to pursue your goals from clarity instead of chaos, and with alignment instead of anxiety. It's what gives you the capacity to take messy, imperfect, courageous action toward the life you actually want, without abandoning yourself along the way.

Before we move into shifting identity or expanding emotional capacity, I want you to pause and really anchor yourself in this skill. When you can recognize what is driving you, take a moment to reflect, and make a conscious choice, something powerful happens. You stop simply chasing goals and start living with awareness and intention. And that kind of pursuit is what truly matters.

And hey, major props for even showing up for this work. Self-reflection is no joke. It's so much easier to scroll Instagram, binge a show, clean your inbox, or alphabetize your spice rack than it is to sit in silence with your own thoughts. Staying busy is easier than getting present. Numbing is easier than feeling. We live in a world that rewards distraction, but awareness takes guts and intention. It takes a willingness to peek under the hood of your inner world and not slam it shut the second something feels unclear or uncomfortable. So, if this feels challenging... good. That means you're doing it right. You're in the arena, and that matters.

I invite you to start small. Give yourself permission to be a beginner. Pick one moment a day and ask yourself: *What am I feeling right now? What thought might be underneath that feeling?* That's it. That's the practice. That's the door to getting started.

In Pursuit Insight:
You don't have to wait for the chaos to calm down to see yourself clearly. Awareness is the calm, and it's available any time you choose to look inward with curiosity instead of judgment.

And remember, self-awareness is not a personality trait. It is not something you either have or don't have. It is a skill you can build. It is a practice you develop. It is a muscle you strengthen through each honest pause, each curious question, and each compassionate response.

Compass Check:
Practice a Thought Download today. Set a timer for five minutes and write what's on your mind. Pick one thought. Run it through the S.T.E.A.R. Model.

Ask yourself:

- What emotion does this thought create?
- How do I act when I feel that way?
- What result does that create?
- What's one alternative thought I could try on—one that feels true, supportive, and aligned with who I want to be?

You are not your thoughts.
You are the thinker, and that makes you powerful.

Want to go deeper?
Scan the QR code to access your free Unblocked Journal. Inside, you'll find guided prompts to help you do a Thought Download and practice the STEAR model in real life.

Story: The Cousin Call from Juvenile Detention

This chapter is all about the things we don't see. It's about the patterns that live beneath the surface and the beliefs we didn't consciously choose. It explores the emotional blueprints we inherited before we even had language. These are the rules etched into our nervous systems from the homes we were raised in and the chaos we learned to normalize. This chapter is about the invisible forces that quietly steer the ship of our lives, until we name them, confront them, and start rewriting the map.

To bring this to life, I want to share a story. It's about how two people can share the same desire and still end up in very different places. This story isn't about discipline or intelligence or being "stronger." It's not about one of us being more motivated or more deserving. This story is about what happens underneath the surface. It's about the unseen blocks, unexamined beliefs, and old wiring that shape our paths, even when we're chasing the same dream.

This story is about my cousin and me. We were born just five days apart to two young, single moms and spent the early years of our lives side by side. We shared a room, toys, clothes, and more than one matching outfit in baby photos. As we got older, we shared weekends at the skating rink, late-night secrets, and a quiet but powerful dream. It wasn't flashy or extravagant by most standards, but for where we came from, it was everything. We made a promise to each other that we weren't going to end up like our moms. That was the dream. Born into a world shaped by teenage motherhood, meth addiction, instability, and incarceration, we imagined something different for ourselves. We didn't know exactly what it would look like, but we knew we wanted something different.

I chased that dream with everything in me. I became the girl who followed all the rules, the one who kept her head down, turned in homework early, smiled when it wasn't safe to speak, tried to make teachers proud, and swallowed her rage before it had the audacity to reach her throat. I wasn't just trying to succeed. I was trying to stay safe. Performance was my currency, and I spent it everywhere I could: straight A's, student council, volunteer hours.

I wore the "good girl" badge like armor, because somewhere along the line, I absorbed a truth that wasn't true but felt like gospel: if I could just be good enough, I'd be safe. I'd be chosen. I'd get out.

The day I graduated as valedictorian of my high school class (a tiny class, so don't be too impressed), I got a phone call. It was a collect call from Juvenile Detention. My cousin was calling to congratulate me. He said he was proud of me for keeping the promise our kid selves had made.

I don't think this happened because I'm better, or stronger, or smarter. I believe it's because I had different tools, different coping strategies, and different forms of support. I had a nervous system that defaulted to perfectionism, a form of hypervigilance that often gets rewarded, instead of fight or flight. I developed internal patterns that helped me funnel fear into achievements, like straight-A papers, instead of street fights or rebellion. We both wanted freedom. We both carried pain. But we didn't both have the same internal scaffolding to escape the gravitational pull of our origin story.

I've spent years trying to make sense of that moment, and this is what I've come to understand: desire is not enough. Willpower is not enough. Motivation is not enough. If your internal blueprint is wired to believe you are not safe unless you hide, perform, rage, sabotage, control, please, or numb, then it doesn't matter how badly you want to be free. Your brain and body will drag you back to what's familiar, even if it hurts, even if it costs you everything.

That's what unconscious programming does. That's what inherited beliefs do. They don't just sit there quietly in your psyche. They pull the strings, until you see them. That's why awareness matters. I'm not talking about awareness like, "I know I procrastinate." This goes beyond surface-level insight to deep, tender, courageous awareness. This kind of awareness asks you to sit with the parts of yourself you've been avoiding. It invites you to meet them without judgment so you can get honest about what's been silently steering your life.

It's easy to tell people to just try harder, choose better, want it more, but that advice only works for people whose internal world is already aligned with the outcome. For the rest of us, for the ones trying to outrun trauma, override scarcity, or decode shame, we have to start by looking inward. We have to learn to spot the blocks before we can begin to shift them. If your inner world is wired in opposition to what you want, you will find a way to sabotage it.

This doesn't happen because you're weak. It happens because of neuroscience. The brain is built for survival and familiarity. Left unsupervised, it will default to both, even if that means working against your growth, your goals, and the life you say you want. You don't need more willpower. You need more awareness. You need to know what you're carrying, whose voice is still living in your head, and which patterns are keeping you stuck. When you name them, you give yourself the power to choose something different.

In Pursuit Insight:
You can't override a belief you've never identified. You can't shift a pattern you haven't seen. Change begins when awareness meets compassion. That's the moment you stop living from programming and start living from choice.

I didn't make it out because I was better. I made it out because I had the tools to see the blocks, and I've made it my life's work to make sure other people get those tools, too.

Chapter 5:

SHIFT the Identity

You're Not Who You Were: Identity Is a Choice, Not a Life Sentence

In my early thirties, I took a cross-country road trip. I had no real agenda, just some playlists, a loose route, and one rule: stop at as many "World's Largest" roadside attractions as I could find. The World's Largest Ball of Twine? Obviously. A massive fiberglass cow? Yes, please. It was kitschy, random, and totally unnecessary, which made it exactly the kind of joy-filled detour I needed at the time.

Somewhere along that zigzag across America, I found myself in Santa Rosa, New Mexico, standing at the edge of the Blue Hole. If you've never been, it's this stunning natural spring that's 80 feet deep, crystal clear, and a constant 62 degrees. For context, you should know that I hate cold water (and cold weather, for that matter). Okay, I just hate to be cold, period. Also, I am absolutely not the person who finds deep, dark, mysterious bodies of water thrilling. In fact, not being able to see the bottom is pretty much a hard pass for me.

Something about that moment—maybe the freedom of the road, too much fresh air, whatever it was—made me pause. I was standing there, fully clothed, and I thought, *What would it be like to be the kind of person who just jumps in?* So I did. I took a deep breath, counted to three, and jumped. Clothes, shoes, all of it. It was shocking. It was freezing. It was exhilarating.

This experience wasn't about bravery or adrenaline. It was about curiosity. Sometimes we do things simply because they're outside our comfort zone, or because we want to know what it feels like to be the version of ourselves who says yes, who jumps, who tries. We want to experience the version of ourselves who doesn't let fear or discomfort be the final decision-maker.

That moment didn't make me a completely different person. It didn't rewrite my résumé or alter my DNA, but it reminded me that identity isn't static. It's fluid, flexible, and full of possibility. The version of me who jumped into that freezing spring wasn't the "real me" or the "new me." She was just a *choice*. She was a version I gave myself permission to meet. And that's what this chapter is about. It's about remembering that you are not cemented into one way of being. Identity is not a static label. It's a living, breathing experience you get to shape on purpose.

You are not a fixed character in a story someone else wrote—not even the one you wrote for yourself. You're not locked into your high school superlative, your Enneagram number, or the survival roles you've learned to play (like achiever, fixer, peacemaker, or perfectionist). You're not who you were five years ago, last month, or even yesterday. And that's not just a feel-good mantra; it's neuroscience. Your brain is built for change. Your identity is far more flexible than you've likely been led to believe.

Your identity isn't a rigid definition. It's a dynamic, multi-layered construct that sits at the intersection of:

1. Who you *believe* you are: your values, memories, preferences, fears, and desires.
2. How you *see* yourself: in relation to others, your roles, affiliations, culture, and power dynamics.
3. And what gives you a sense of continuity over time: your narrative, purpose, and meaning.

Here's the radical invitation: you can shape that identity on purpose. You can change the story, not to escape who you were, but to become who you actually are underneath the survival scripts.

By now, you've probably started to notice some of those invisible prisons you've been living in. You've begun to name the patterns, to question the roles, and to observe the inner voices whispering, "*Be good,*" "*Don't mess it up,*" or "*This is just how I am.*" That awareness is powerful, but it's not the transformation. It's the beginning of the shift, not the end of the story.

If you want to stop repeating patterns that don't serve you...

If you want to stop saying yes to things that drain you...

If you want to finally begin that project you've been dreaming about for years...

You don't just need more motivation. You need to shift the identity that's driving the behavior.

This is where we start talking about the *who*.

One of my former mentors used to say, *"The first step isn't figuring out the how. It's becoming the who."* For most of us, the minute we want to change something, we reach for the strategy. We ask, *"What do I need to do?"* or *"What's the right system?"* But underneath every system lives a story, a belief, an identity that either supports the change, or silently resists it.

That can be particularly problematic when going after a goal or doing something we've never done before because many of us define ourselves–and what's possible–based on what we've always done:

"I'm someone who always runs late."
"I've never been consistent."
"I have to be right."
"I need everything to be perfect."

We say these things like facts. But they're not facts, they're familiar, practiced, habituated protections.

Much of what we call "personality" is actually just a blend of stories, roles, and reactions we adopted to feel safe, accepted, or in control.

You became the responsible one because someone had to be.

You became an achiever because it gave you a way to matter.

You became the quiet one because attention never felt safe.

You became the peacekeeper because conflict always led to chaos.

Those patterns weren't your personality. They were your armor. That armor may have protected you then, but it could also be what's holding you back now. Most people don't pause long enough to recognize when the armor is no longer needed. It doesn't fall off on its own. You have to notice it, name it, and make the conscious decision to loosen your grip when it no longer serves you. In case no one has told you, it's okay to let it go. It might be safe now. You don't have to keep being who you had to be.

Shifting your identity isn't about becoming someone fake. It's not about abandoning who you've been. It's about asking better questions. Instead of *"What should I do next?"* or *"What goal should I chase now?"* try asking, *"Who is the version of me who has already achieved the goal I'm working toward?"* *"How do they think, feel, and show up?"* or *"What parts of me do I want to explore more fully?"* The "how" will flow from the "who."

This is where a lot of people get stuck. They jump straight into strategy but eventually burn out trying to force action that's misaligned with their current identity. Remember, belief drives behavior, thank you, S.T.E.A.R. Model. If you still see yourself as someone who "never follows through," your brain will subtly resist consistency, no matter how many productivity hacks you stack. If your identity is wrapped up in being liked, you'll self-sabotage anything that risks disapproval. This doesn't happen because you're lazy or lack willpower. It happens because your subconscious is in a tug-of-war between who you say you want to be and who you still believe you are.

One of my clients used to say, *"I always get projects 60% done and never finish."* So, of course, that's exactly what she kept creating. When we looked beneath the surface, we uncovered a deeper belief: *"The only way to get things done is to white-knuckle and bulldog my way through it."* Consciously, she wanted to approach her work with more ease and grace. But subconsciously, she believed that results only came through struggle and force. Once we identified that belief, she could begin trying on a new identity: *"I'm someone who completes tasks with grace, ease, fulfillment, and satisfaction."* And with that shift, her results started to change.

This chapter is about that shift. We're going beneath the goals, routines, and habits. We're looking at the identity level, because that's where lasting change lives. We're going to talk about how identity is shaped, how it forms, how it sticks, and how to begin choosing it on purpose. To be clear, this isn't about "fixing" yourself or becoming a "better" version of yourself. This is about stepping into a truer version of yourself–the version of you who already knows how to live the life you want. They're not some fantasy. They already exist. You've probably already met that version of you in the quiet moments, in the dreams you've pushed aside, and in the ways you light up when no one's watching. They're not a future goal. They're already present within you. They just might be buried under layers of blocks and old programming.

You've probably heard the idea that if you want to achieve something big, you need to start acting "as if." That's true, but let's take it deeper. It's not just about acting like your future self. It's about *thinking* like them, *feeling* like them, and *believing* what they believe. How you define yourself today and who you choose to become is ultimately up to you. You can choose what to believe about yourself. You can choose the meaning you make of your past. You can choose the future version of yourself you are stepping into.

So, here's where we're headed. We are moving from simply understanding identity to fully inhabiting it. We are shifting from naming the blocks to becoming the kind of person who moves through them. You're going to learn how to bridge the gap between who you've been and who you're becoming. You'll do that using simple but powerful tools like visualization, conscious decision-making, and micro-alignment. These practices will support you in living as if your future self is already here.

This is the moment in your journey where you stop trying to change from the outside in, and start transforming from the inside out.

You stop asking, *"What should I do?"* Instead, you start asking, *"Who am I becoming?"*
You ask, *"What does that version of me choose?"*
And, *"How do they move through the world?"*

In Pursuit Insight:
The question isn't, *"What should I do?"* The better question is, *"What do I truly want?"* The difference is key. Aligned desire is the compass that leads to a life that doesn't just look good, but feels like yours. When you shift from chasing expectations to choosing what resonates, you stop performing life and start inhabiting it. That's the real success story.

The version of you who lives with ease, freedom, and fulfillment isn't someone you have to find. It's a part of you to remember, and it's time to meet them.

Compass Check:
Ask yourself:

- What identity have I unconsciously been living from?
- What would shift if I stopped calling it my "personality" and started seeing it as practiced protection?
- Who do I want to be now, and what small action could I take today to live from that place?

Write your answers. Speak them out loud. Revisit them often. Every choice you make is a vote for the identity you're stepping into. Let this be the chapter where you remember that identity isn't a life sentence. It's a conscious choice.

The Who Before the How: Becoming the Aligned You

What I'm about to say might sound like I'm coming in hot. Maybe I am. I'm not here to coddle the part of you that keeps playing small. I'm here as a zealous advocate for your highest self, and for the version of you that already knows who they are and is just waiting for you to catch up. So let me say this clearly: if you don't believe you're the kind of person who does the thing, whatever your thing is, you will keep talking yourself out of doing it. This is true, whether your dream is finding an extraordinary partner, building a Fortune 50 company, writing a *New York Times* bestseller, or winning an Olympic medal in figure skating. Without belief, you will fall short. Full stop.

That's the real trap. It's not the wrong strategy. It's not a lack of discipline. It's not even a shortage of time. The true source of friction is internal. You can't build a life that aligns with your future self if your identity is still anchored in your past. You can't bring your whole self to the table if any part of you still believes you don't belong there.

Identity is upstream of behavior. It's the *who* that drives the *how*. If you believe you're bad with money, you'll keep "accidentally" overdrafting your account. If you believe you're not a real writer, you'll clean your kitchen ten times before you ever sit down at the keyboard.

Here's what's wild: even if you push through and take action, if your self-concept hasn't shifted, you'll experience the whole thing as if you're an impostor. That kind of dissonance makes everything feel twice as heavy and half as effective. And worse, it robs you of joy. It steals the very experience you're working so hard to have.

You can train for a marathon, write a book, launch a business, and still say, *"I'm not really the kind of person who does this."* So instead of seeing yourself as someone becoming, someone in process, and someone living the dream in real time, you stay stuck in the purgatory of *trying*. And trying always implies distance, like the goal is still out of reach. Trying keeps you in the gap, and when you're in the gap, you're always chasing, never arriving. This is why changing your habits isn't enough. If your identity doesn't evolve with your actions, you will eventually self-sabotage just to stay consistent with your outdated self-story. The brain craves consistency. It wants what is familiar, even if what's familiar is dysfunctional, misaligned, or self-sabotaging.

So, let me ask you plainly, who do you believe you are?

Do you believe you're someone who finishes what they start?

Or maybe you're someone who does hard things with ease and doesn't make it mean anything about their worth?

Do you believe your voice matters—that people are waiting on the edge of their seats for the next thing you're about to say, do, or create?

Do you believe you are worthy of success that feels good?

Do you believe you're even capable of success?

If you don't, then it doesn't matter how many productivity hacks you implement or tools you try, you'll burn out trying to live a life that's out of sync with who you still believe you are. This is where the reclamation begins.

When I ran a marathon, I was not what anyone would call "a runner." I didn't look like a runner. I didn't have the expensive watch, the perfect form, or the elite hydration strategy dialed in. I wasn't part of a running group or a Strava gang. I didn't run to meditate or find myself. I ran because I made a decision. I wanted to run 26.2 miles without walking or stopping. Just me, my stubborn resolve, and a pair of wildly average shoes.

And you know what? I did it. I ran that whole dang marathon without stopping and even placed tenth in my age group. Now, that doesn't land me on any Olympic podium. But y'all, this "non-runner" beat out a lot of people who probably did consider themselves runners. I ran the miles. I crossed the finish line. I proved to myself I could do something hard.

And yet, when people asked me about the race afterward, do you know what came out of my mouth? *"Oh, no no no. I'm not a runner."*

Excuse me? I had literally just done the thing runners do: *run*. I even ran far. But still, I disqualified myself from the identity. I had to pause and question the absurdity of that. What invisible metric was I holding up that said I could do the thing but still not *be* the thing?

As I got curious, here's what I found. In my mind, "runners" were tall and sinewy. They had specialized gear and strategic gels. They wore compression socks and had ovals on their SUVs that read "26.2." They got high off the movement. They were in the club. They were so committed to the sport, and I cannot believe I'm saying this, that they'd literally risk shitting their pants mid-race just to keep their pace. Y'all. This is why we supervise our brains.

And the deeper I looked, the more I saw the function of this disqualifying rubric. If I wasn't "really" a runner, then I didn't have to take myself seriously. I didn't have to meet expectations. I didn't have to be proud of myself or own my effort. I could protect myself from failure and visibility and just keep saying, *"Oh, I'm just doing this for fun."* But guess what? That line of thinking robs us of the experience we're already in. It cuts us off from the joy of becoming.

What if I *am* a runner? What if runners can be people who run, period? What if you don't have to be a certain weight or pace or have a sticker on your car to claim the identity? When I let myself believe I was a runner, something clicked. Running became lighter, more playful. I stopped keeping a mental scoreboard and started enjoying the process. I got curious about what else I'd been telling myself I'm not. If I was wrong about not being a runner, where else might I be wrong about myself?

You don't have to be the "best" version of a thing to belong to it. You don't need a panel of judges to approve your application for a new identity. You just have to show up and do the thing. Then do it again. Until one day, you realize the thing you were trying to become, you've already been. That's the quiet miracle of identity shift. It happens the moment you whisper: *"Maybe I am."*

Maybe I *am* a writer.
Maybe I *am* a runner.
Maybe I *am* a leader.
Maybe I *am* loved.

When you let yourself believe that it's even possible, that someone like *you* could be that, you don't just dream it. You begin to live it and be it.

When I started this book, my brain offered the same nonsense. *"You're not a writer."* I had ideas, sure, but in my head, writers were tortured souls sipping espresso in bookstore cafés, spinning metaphors from pain like alchemists. That wasn't me, but here I am, writing a book. At some point, you stop asking if you fit someone else's mold and start asking if you *feel the pull*. That's the shift. That's where possibility lives. It's not about fitting someone else's idea of what "*that kind of person*" looks like. It's about deciding that your version gets to count too.

Maybe runners look like people in baggy shirts with playlists from 2007.

Maybe writers are women who scribble in notebooks between carpool lines.

Maybe CEOs cry in bathroom stalls before Zoom calls and still run empires.

Maybe people like us do things we were never given permission to do, and we do them anyway.

And just in case this is coming up for you, let me offer that you don't need to ask anyone for permission to become the kind of person who does the thing you want to do. You get to give that to yourself. If no one has told you, hear it now: you're allowed to want what you want, even if no one claps, even if no one else gets it yet.

This is about reclaiming and redefining what it means to be the good mom, the great dad, the high achiever, the creative, the successful one. Maybe your version doesn't look like what you saw growing up or what Instagram tries to sell you, but it doesn't mean it's not valid. You don't have to mimic someone else's version to be the real deal. You just have to claim yours.

That's where belief comes in—real, grounded, practiced belief. This isn't about blind optimism or sticky-note affirmations that feel fake. I'm talking about belief as a skill you cultivate, like a muscle. You don't start with certainty. You start with willingness. You say, "*Maybe it's possible. Maybe this gets to be for me, too.*" And then you take one aligned action, and then another.

Belief is built by shifting thoughts and aligning feelings and actions to the version of you who knows it's already true. So, if you want to be a runner, run—slowly and in old sneakers. If you want to be a writer, write; do it messily and in the notes app on your phone. If you want to build a business, start; do it scared, with a free Canva logo and an offer that's still half-formed.

This isn't about faking it 'til you make it. It's about recognizing that if you have the dream, you already have the raw materials to bring it to life. Just like an acorn already contains everything it needs to grow into an oak tree, you've already got what it takes inside of you. The potential is there. Your job isn't to become someone else, it's to nurture what's already yours.

Stop waiting to feel ready. Start showing up like the version of you who knows it's possible… because it is. You already *are* someone who can do the thing. You just have to stop looking for the version that's palatable, acceptable, or polished enough, and start becoming the version that's true.

Let's reclaim the title, the dream, and the next chapter.

You get to be someone who _____. Fill in the blank. No disclaimers. No detours. No delay.

In Pursuit Insight:
You don't have to become someone else. You just have to stop disqualifying yourself from being who you already are.

If belief feels out of reach, let me offer you a tool that helps access the next version of yourself. It's called *The Alter Ego Effect*, and was coined by peak performance coach Todd Herman, who teaches that you don't need to *wait* to feel like the person who can show up powerfully. You can step into an intentional identity now by channeling an "alter ego." This is a version of yourself who already has the traits, courage, or mindset you need. It's not pretending. It's accessing a part of you that already exists but may have been buried under fear, conditioning, or the need to please.

Athletes, CEOs, and creators use this all the time. Beyoncé created "Sasha Fierce" to help her own the stage. You can create your own alter ego, too. This isn't pretending. It's practice. It's accessing what's already inside you but got buried under years of shame, socialization, or self-protection.

Try This Exercise: Build Your Alter Ego
If the idea of showing up "as if" feels abstract or out of reach, meet your new favorite tool: the Alter Ego. This tool helps you call forward a version of yourself who already exists–the bold, grounded, get-it-done version who's just waiting for permission to lead.

Step 1: Define the Identity

Think about the goal or behavior you're working toward. Who's the version of you who already does the thing with confidence? Give them a name if it helps. (Yes, I'm serious.) You can call them Audacious Alice, Bold Brad, or simply The Version Who Knows. I call my CEO alter ego Penelope Powerhouse. Don't judge me, I love a good alliteration.

Step 2: Describe Them

How do they walk? Talk? Make decisions? What do they believe about themselves? Write it out. Make them real.

Step 3: Anchor It

Pick a small "activation ritual" that helps you switch into your alter ego. It could be a playlist, a piece of jewelry or clothing, or a scent, anything that helps you access them on demand.

Step 4: Practice

Let them show up today. Let them run the meeting, write the post, or send the pitch. Pay attention to how it feels.

Again, you're not faking it. You're remembering what's already inside you. The Alter Ego just helps you get there faster.

All the stuff I'm talking about here–questioning old rubrics, claiming new ones, daring to believe you can belong to your own desire–isn't just theory. This is about real life. Let me show you what I mean.

I want to tell you about one of the hardest and most courageous decisions I have ever made. It wasn't a decision about logistics or timing or strategy. It was a decision about identity. It was a decision that forced me to ask, *"Who am I, really? What do I actually want? And what kind of life am I willing to live that aligns with that truth?"*

Years ago, I was married to a really good man. He was kind, steady, and honest. He treated me *really* well, with devoted care and respect. He came from a beautiful, connected, emotionally healthy family. The kind of family that cooks together, checks in regularly, hugs with full presence. We had a good life. We made real memories, and for a while, that was enough. But underneath the "good," the rightness on paper, something in me felt off. Like an instrument that looks polished but plays just slightly out of tune. I couldn't explain it. There was no betrayal, no dramatic blow-up. There was just a quiet, growing sense of misalignment that I couldn't shake.

Then he got offered a tenure-track job across the country. He suggested we go. I felt like the alarm bells went off. I couldn't breathe. I didn't feel ready. I didn't want to leave my job, my career. He offered to go alone, to test it out temporarily, and I felt myself exhale for the first time in weeks. That's when I started to know something wasn't right. After considering this option for a while, he came back and said, *"I'd rather work at Burger King and see my wife every day than take a dream job without you."*

It gutted me that I didn't feel the same. I didn't want to go. I didn't want to build that version of a life, and he deserved someone who did. I didn't leave because he failed me. I left because we couldn't give each other what we really needed.

And the hardest part was, there was no villain. There was no external justification. I remember thinking, *I wish there had been abuse or infidelity.* At least then this would be easier to explain; at least then it would feel acceptable. But there wasn't. There was just truth, and truth was enough. It had to be.

I was also deeply embarrassed. I felt like I had broken the "good girl" rules. I felt like I had betrayed some silent code of what a "grateful woman" does. I didn't tell people at work. I kept his last name, partly for the convenience (have you ever tried updating professional licenses and email signatures?!), but partly because I thought a name change would reveal the secret. It would scream, *She got divorced. She didn't make it work. She gave up something good.*

But here's what I know now. I didn't leave a good marriage to chase a shiny new life. I left to reclaim myself. I left to stop pretending. I left to be honest. And that, more than anything, is what identity shift demands of us. You don't rewrite your story by burning it down. You rewrite it by telling the truth about who you are now, even if it costs you the version of life you thought you were supposed to live.

I'm not sharing this story because I think you should leave your relationship or your job or your city. I share it because you deserve permission to tell the truth about what fits and what doesn't, about what's alive and what's not, about what's aligned and what's been outgrown. Sometimes the boldest, most loving thing you can do for yourself and others is say, *"This version of me doesn't belong here anymore,"* and then let go.

I'll never forget when one of my mentors went through a public divorce. Her husband wasn't just her partner in life; he was also her business partner. So, when things ended, everyone had questions. Someone finally asked her,

"Why are you getting a divorce?" Her answer, *"I've answered this question, and people just don't like the answer. I'm getting a divorce...because I want to."*

Y'all.

Because. I. Want. To.

I remember hearing that and thinking, *dang. That's a different level of self-concept. That's sovereignty. That's self-permission.* She wasn't defending, explaining, or justifying. She was someone who gave herself permission to want what she wanted and act on it, even when it's not easy, even when no one is clapping.

So, let me pass that on to you.

You are allowed to want what you want. You are allowed to leave what no longer fits. You are allowed to walk away from good things that are no longer *your* things. You are allowed to stop performing a role and start living your truth.

You don't have to earn it. It doesn't have to look good on paper or make sense to anyone else. You get to pivot because it's aligned to you. That's reason enough.

Compass Check:
Ask yourself:

- What's one identity I've been holding onto that no longer serves me?
- What version of me am I becoming?
- How would that version of me speak, decide, or show up today?
- What are three things that version of me believes?
- Where am I already being this version in small, overlooked ways?

Choose one area of your life (work, relationships, wellness, etc.) and ask:

- What would change if I stopped saying *"I'm not that kind of person"* and started saying *"I'm someone who..."*?

Build the Belief to Back It Up: Tool to Take Action From the "Who"

It's one thing to imagine a new version of yourself. It's another to actually believe you can become them. Identity work without belief doesn't activate real change. It just sounds good on paper. Without belief, nothing sticks. You'll keep circling the same goals, wondering why your strategies aren't working. It's not working because, at the root, your subconscious is still playing by the old rules. That's why this work matters. Shifting into a new identity isn't just about how you talk or what you wear, it's about what you believe to be true about who you are and what's possible for you.

And here's the good news: belief isn't something you're born with or without. It's not reserved for the ultra-confident, the genetically optimistic, or TikTok coaches with ring lights and morning routines. Belief is a skill. It can be practiced, built, and strengthened, just like anything else.

A lot of people come to me frustrated that their spouse, their family, their boss, their team, or their audience doesn't believe in them. While I have compassion for that pain, I always offer the same hard truth: *"If you want someone to believe in you... you go first."* I know. Ouch. But I don't leave them hanging there. I actually teach them how to do it. I teach them how to build belief from the inside out, and that's what I want to offer you now.

Building belief is a practice. It's a process of intentionally choosing which thoughts you'll feed, which patterns you'll prune, and what version of yourself you'll water.

Let's start with the beliefs you're currently holding, especially the ones that aren't serving you. Thoughts like *"I'm not consistent,"* or *"I never finish what I start,"* or *"People like me don't build businesses like that"* don't sound like dramatic identity statements, but they are. Those thoughts are decisions your brain made, usually in a moment of fear, failure, or shame, and now they've calcified into what feels like truth. But they're not the truth. They're just practiced, rehearsed, and familiar.

The only reason you deeply believe something is simply because you've thought it so many times. Here's the power in that idea. If a belief is just a thought you've practiced, then you can un-practice it. You can replace it. You can retrain your brain to believe something better. You are one thought away from creating your desired results. Let's teach you the skills to find and cultivate that thought.

This is where I want to introduce you to additional skills that help you *Think On Purpose*, or T.O.P., because I love an acronym. You learned about Thought Downloads and the S.T.E.A.R. Model in Chapter 4. Those T.O.P. skills help bring awareness to what you're currently thinking and what you create with those beliefs. Now I want to introduce some tools that will help build new beliefs.

One of the tools is P.D.T.: *Purposefully Derived Thoughts*. Yes, I know that's a mouthful, hence the acronym. #WeLoveAcronyms.

The idea behind P.D.T. is to stop waiting for a new belief to drop in from the sky, and start consciously choosing what you want to believe.

The first step of P.D.T. is to find the places where belief already exists, even in small ways. Let's say you're working on the belief *"I'm someone who follows through."* Your brain might want to roll its eyes. *"Uh, no, you're not. We have evidence."* Instead of arguing with the brain, we invite it to look closer. Did you show up for work today? Did you keep a promise to a friend? Did you finish something small this week—a workout, a book, a commitment? Then there it is: a foothold, a flicker. You don't have to fake belief. You just have to amplify what's already true.

Here are some P.D.T. prompts to help your brain get on board with belief-building:

- What do I already know?
- What *is* clear?
- Where do I agree, even a little?
- How might this be true already?
- In what ways do I *like* this idea?
- Why would this belief serve me?
- How could this add value, joy, or ease to my life?

Let your answers surprise you. Let them soften you. Let them give your nervous system something solid to rest on, because this next tool is where it all starts to take root. It's called the *Thought Ladder.*[3]

---

[3] The concepts I share here are based on, and/or built on, tools I learned through Brooke Castillo and The Life Coach School Certification Program.

This is where we build belief one rung at a time.

Instead of leaping from *"I'm terrible with money"* to *"I'm a financial wizard,"* which your brain will reject as nonsense, you take small, believable steps. If you tell your brain something it doesn't believe, it will dig in its heels and resist. However, if you offer a small and believable shift, something that feels just a bit more empowering, real belief change can take root.

So instead of forcing yourself to say, *"I'm amazing with money,"* start with:

- *"Maybe I could get a little better at this."*
- *"It's possible I'm wrong about being bad with money."*
- *"I'm open to believing it's possible I could be smarter with money."*
- *It's possible I could become someone who makes smart financial decisions."*

The goal is to find a thought that feels *slightly better* (or even less terrible) and more *energizing* than the one before it. If your body softens, your breath deepens, or something inside you whispers, *"yes,"* you're on the right track.

If you try on a new thought and feel nothing, it's not a problem. It just means you tried to take too big of a step on the ladder. Simply go down a rung and try a thought that's closer to the previous one. When the new "rung" becomes your default thought, then you know it's time to work your way to the next rung. Then you keep repeating that until you reach your desired belief.

Since I'm full of all the good news, let me tell you, belief alone won't get you where you want to go. You can't just sit on your couch visualizing greatness and expect your life to magically rearrange itself. Belief matters, but belief *in motion* is what changes things.

This is where micro-alignment comes in. Think of it as belief in action.

Micro-alignment means choosing small, purposeful actions that match the identity you're stepping into. If you're cultivating the belief *"I'm a person who honors her time,"* maybe today that means saying no to a request that drains you. If you're building the identity *"I'm a business owner who shows up consistently,"* maybe you reach out to five different people today to talk about your business and how it might help them. These small moves compound.

If you want to reverse-engineer a new outcome, the S.T.E.A.R. Model is your blueprint. Start with the end in mind. What's the *Result* you want to create? Then ask yourself what consistent *Actions* would generate that result. What *Emotion* would I need to feel in order to take those actions consistently? What *Thought* would naturally produce that emotion?

It's like programming a GPS for your brain. The same action can produce wildly different results depending on what thought and emotion you're plugging into the action.

One of the best analogies I've heard about belief-fueled action involved a fire truck. Imagine *Action* as a fire truck. Now, imagine fueling that fire truck with firefighters, meaning thoughts like, *"This matters. I've got what it takes."* You're going to get a focused, effective result.

In Pursuit Insight

Belief is a skill, not a feeling. You don't have to feel ready. You just have to be willing.

Now imagine sending that same fire truck to a fire, but instead of trained firefighters, it's filled with kindergartners. In this case, the kindergartners represent thoughts like, *"This won't work,"* or *"I'm terrible at this."* You're going to get a very different outcome, and a totally different result.

If your actions are infused with doubt, fear, or scarcity, it won't land the way you want it to. But if it's backed by a belief that aligns with the version of you that you're becoming, that's when momentum kicks in. That's when the work feels less like a grind and more like fulfillment, satisfaction, and fun.

Visualization is another powerful amplifier. Not in a woo-woo, *close-your-eyes-and-hope-for-a-miracle* kind of way, but as a neurological rehearsal. When you visualize the version of you who already has what you want, whether it's the business, the relationship, or the inner peace, your brain starts to normalize that reality.

If you tried on an alter ego in the last section, you've already tasted this. Giving your future self a name or persona helps your brain practice *being* them, even before the belief is fully integrated. It's mental reps, and eventually, what started as a performance becomes embodiment.

That's the magic of belief. What starts as *"maybe"* becomes *"of course."* You don't have to fully believe it yet. You just need to believe enough to take the next step, and then the next. With every move you make, the identity you're building gets more real, until one day, you're not *trying* to be that version anymore.

You just *are*.

Remember, you're not here to chase someone else's dream. You're here to become the version of you who is fully alive inside the one you're already living. The shifts aren't just in your goals, they're in your sense of self. And when that shifts, everything follows.

Compass Check:
Ask yourself:

- What's a belief I've been rehearsing that no longer serves me?
- What's a new belief I want to cultivate?
- Where is that belief *already* a little true?
- What's a one-rung-higher thought I *can* believe today?
- What's one small action I could take that aligns with this new belief?

Then, take it. That's how it becomes real, not all at once, but one belief-backed move at a time.

Chapter 6:

STAY with the Emotions

Emotional Presence: Feel it to Free it

I once threw a glass bowl across the room. I was probably fourteen or fifteen at the time. I had a varsity softball game that day. I also had my eight-year-old brother with me, and I couldn't find my parents. I stood there, gear in hand, watching the team bus pull away without me. I couldn't leave him, so I missed the game.

I wouldn't have described myself as an angry teen. I was responsible, probably overly so. I was the one who made it to practice, turned in homework early, remembered permission slips, and knew how to read the room. I kept things buttoned up and kept myself regulated, because someone had to. But after missing my game that day, I was decidedly unregulated.

Throwing my mom's glass crafting bowl against the cinder block basement wall didn't just shatter the bowl. It shattered the illusion that I was okay. The rage wasn't about the bowl. It wasn't even just about that moment. It was everything that had been left unfelt, unspoken, unprocessed—a silent load of frustration, sadness, disappointment, and loneliness all crashing through my body in one loud, violent exhale. That bowl just happened to be in the way.

What I've come to understand, and what I wish someone had taught me years earlier, is that unprocessed emotion doesn't disappear. It stores. It waits. It gets heavy. And eventually, it leaks, or explodes, or festers into anxiety, disconnection, and self-sabotage. Most of us were never taught how to *feel* our feelings. We were taught how to suppress them, mask them, or repackage them into something more palatable.

Smile.
Stay positive.
Don't cry.
Don't be dramatic.
Be grateful.
Move on.

But if you're reading this book, you already know the truth. You know that numbing out doesn't lead to peace; it just delays the pain. You know that powering through isn't the same as healing. You know that some part of you is tired of pretending to be fine when your body and soul are saying otherwise. You're ready to feel—not to fall apart, but to finally fall into alignment.

There's a reason I titled this chapter *"Stay."* That reason is because most of us are incredibly skilled at running. We run from discomfort with distraction. We run from fear with control. We run from vulnerability with humor, sarcasm, perfectionism, or performance. But the true path to freedom, the real, sustainable, deeply rooted kind, requires presence.

Presence demands that we stay. It requires us to stay in the room with our experience. It invites us to stay with the emotions that make us want to crawl out of our own skin. It asks us to stay with the sensations in the body long enough to hear what they're trying to say. It challenges us to stay with the emotion long enough to learn that it's just a temporary sensation, not something to fear or escape. Emphasis on the *temporary*.

Let me show you what that looks like in real life. I was floating in the pool, book in hand, fully relaxed on my adult lounge floaty. It was one of those rare, blissful moments where everything felt still. My husband Joe opened the back door and let our 85-pound goldendoodle, PJ, outside. I called out, *"Grab him before he jumps in the pool."* Joe, ever the optimist, smiled and said, *"He's perfect. He won't do that."*

You can probably guess what happened next. PJ got excited (like, full-body-wiggle excited) and launched straight into the pool. Chaos erupted. I started yelling for Joe to come help. But instead of springing into action, he stood calmly at the edge, unfazed. Meanwhile, I was scrambling in the water, wrangling our soggy, heavy dog and dragging him out of the pool. I was livid. I stomped inside and slammed the door behind me. Definitely not my most grounded moment.

But here's the thing, I didn't stop at the tantrum. I took a breath and paused, for literally 30 seconds. I let the anger move through me like a vibration. I let it burn, rise, then settle without analyzing, judging, or trying to fix it.

And when it passed, so did the emotional charge. I could see the moment differently. It was inconvenient and messy, sure, but not catastrophic. It wasn't something that warranted ruining the rest of our afternoon. A past version of me would've stewed in that unprocessed anger, replaying the moment, justifying my irritation, and staying disconnected from my husband for hours, maybe even the rest of the day.

But this time was different because I *stayed* with the emotion instead of stuffing it or spiraling in it. I was able to come back to myself, and back to connection, faster. That's the power of staying with the emotion.

Many of my clients tell me they're afraid that if they sit with an emotion, they will get swallowed up by it and won't be able to get out. I promise you won't, and the only way to know that for yourself is to *stay* and experience it.

When you resist, react to, or avoid a feeling, you often create more suffering than the emotion itself ever could. But when you stay, you start to see that the feeling will pass, that it's manageable, and that it doesn't define you. You are not your emotions. You're the one experiencing them.

Staying with emotion is a practice. It's a skill. And like any skill, it can be learned.

This isn't about wallowing or dramatizing or drowning in your feelings. It's about creating enough space between you and your emotion that you can see it clearly, hold it gently, and let it move through you. That's what emotions are meant to do, *move*. They are energy in motion. They're not problems to be solved. They are messengers to be heard. To help with this, I use a practice I call S.P.A.C.E. It's not a checklist. It's an invitation to stay present with yourself instead of defaulting to old patterns of resistance, avoidance, or reactivity.

The S.P.A.C.E. Practice: A 5-Step Framework for Feeling Your Feelings

S: Sense the Emotion. Start by identifying and sensing the emotion. I know it sounds basic, but in a world that rewards numbing and constant motion, it's often the hardest step. In order to truly sense what you're feeling, you need to slow your roll long enough to notice and name it.

Get as specific as you can. Emotional granularity is the name of the game. Maybe you're calling it sadness, but is it actually disappointment, grief, or despair? Is the anger actually betrayal, resentment, or powerlessness?

If you need help, grab a feelings wheel. Seriously. It's not silly, it's smart. It can help you find the word that most accurately describes the sensation in your body. If you can't quite pinpoint exactly what you're feeling, that's okay too. Simply acknowledging *"I'm having a feeling"* is a solid place to start. You don't have to nail it perfectly. You just have to get honest.

P: Permission to Feel. Once you've named the emotion, the next step is giving yourself permission to feel it. This is where self-compassion stops being a nice idea and becomes a non-negotiable.

Most of us are pros at judging ourselves for how we feel. We try to rationalize it away, shame ourselves out of it, or scold our nervous system into "calming down" like it's a misbehaving toddler in a grocery store. But emotional maturity begins when we stop abandoning ourselves in the name of composure.

Giving yourself permission to feel is like saying, *"You're safe with me."* It's reminding yourself that no emotion is bad, and none of them make you weak, broken, or unlovable. It's choosing to stay with yourself when things feel hard instead of bailing on yourself emotionally. It's saying to yourself, *"This is uncomfortable, but I'm willing to be with you anyway."* The root of emotional resilience is learning to be with yourself when things feel hard.

The compassionate permission slip might sound like:

"This is hard, and I'm allowed to feel it."
"You're safe with me."
"I'm willing to feel anything if it means staying with you."
"This sensation is intense, and I'm willing to feel this so that you can be known."

Let the feeling know it belongs, and that you won't abandon yourself this time.

A: Awareness in the Body. Now we move into the body, because awareness isn't just cognitive, it's also somatic. Our emotions speak through physical sensations. If we want to feel them fully, we have to stop intellectualizing and start noticing.

Ask yourself, *"Where is this feeling in my body?"* That's a powerful question to start with because it gets you out of your head and into your body.

A body scan can help. Start at the top of your head and slowly move your awareness down your body like you're shining a flashlight over every inch of you. As you mentally scan your body, pay attention to where you feel any sensation. Is there tightness in your throat? Is your chest heavy? Is there a knot in your belly or a buzz in your legs?

Remember, this isn't about fixing anything. You're here to witness the sensations. Your only job is to notice what's happening in your body and let it be exactly what it is.

C: Compassionate Witnessing. Now comes the part that trips most people up: *compassionate witnessing.*

This is where we usually short-circuit because our brains go straight into fix-it mode. We want to do something, solve it, control it, suppress it, move it along as fast as possible. But what if that's not your job right now? What if your only job is to notice, breathe, soften, and stay?

Allowing an emotion means letting go of judgment and stepping into the role of curious observer. That's it. The moment you stop resisting, something miraculous happens. The emotion begins to move. What felt stuck starts to shift. What felt unbearable becomes manageable. What felt terrifying becomes tolerable, because you're no longer fighting it. You're allowing it. And in that allowance, you access a deeper kind of strength.

Remember, emotions are just visitors. They don't need you to build them a house or give them a job. They just want to pass through. You don't have to rush them, judge them, or "do it right." As cliché as it sounds, feelings just want to be felt.

This is the part of the process where you get curious about emotions. Describe it in detail. Where is it? What is the temperature, texture, and movement? Is it hot or cold? Is it hard or soft? Is it still or buzzing?

If you were going to teach someone what this emotion feels like, how would you teach it? Imagine you were describing it to a Martian who had no idea what a human emotion feels like. How would you describe sadness, shame, or rage? The more sensory-specific you get, the better.

E: Expansion. The final step is expansion. This is where you let the emotion move all the way through. Your mind is going to be blown by how fast this can happen.

When you witness the sensation in your body without resisting or overthinking, sometimes it can pass in as little as ten seconds. *Ten seconds!* If it takes longer, that's okay too. Emotions don't work on your timeline. It gets to take as long as it takes.

Just remember this. If you can keep your brain from interfering, the body will process the vibration of an emotion much quicker. So, give yourself permission to notice the sensation and witness it. Let it be there without judgment. Then, watch it move through you. Watch it come and go like a wave.

This is where freedom begins. As you allow the emotion to exist without resistance, you create room for the next layer of awareness. With your nervous system regulated, your prefrontal cortex (aka your wise decision-maker) comes back online. Now you can think more clearly and choose more consciously.

Once you've fully felt the feeling using the S.P.A.C.E. method, you're back in your body, grounded and clear. You're no longer hijacked. You can breathe and think straight. And from this steady place, you can explore new possibilities and move forward with intention.

This is where the F.R.E.E. framework enters the chat. It's my go-to for taking aligned action after you've regulated your emotions.

S.P.A.C.E. helps you stay present with yourself. F.R.E.E. helps you move forward without abandoning yourself. (Yes, I know. *Another* acronym. But, hey, I love them, and they work.)

F.R.E.E.: From Emotional Presence to Aligned Action

F is for FACTS. The first step is to separate facts from the story you're telling about them. I won't lie, this part can be tricky, especially when you're caught in a swirl of emotion. But this step is essential.

Facts are neutral. They're objective. They don't come with emotional weight. Everything else, including the meaning you assign to those facts, is story.

"She disrespected me."
"I always fail."
"This shouldn't have happened."

None of those are facts. They're interpretations. Even though they feel true, that doesn't make them *truth*. Emotions are real and valid, but feelings aren't facts. Neither are thoughts.

When you can pull apart the facts from the narrative, you create enough distance to loosen the emotional grip. That doesn't mean your story is wrong. It just means it's optional. And if it's optional, it's also changeable.

That's really good news, especially if the current version of the story isn't serving you.

R is for RELEASE. Once you've clarified the facts, you can move into releasing the emotional charge that's still lingering in your body. This is what the tools from S.P.A.C.E. help with: identifying the emotion, offering yourself compassion, tuning into your body, observing the sensations, and allowing the emotion to move through.

Release is *not* the same as suppression.

This step isn't about pretending you're fine. It's not *"get over it"* or *"just move on."* It's a conscious and compassionate process of letting your body complete the emotional cycle. Most people get stuck because they try to skip this part.

But when you feel it, you free it.

Release creates the internal room you need in order to access your creativity, clarity, and power.

E is for EXPLORE. Once your nervous system has calmed and your mind is grounded in reality, you're ready to get curious. This is the fun part. Ask yourself:

- What else might be true?
- What else might be possible?

- What do I *actually* want here?
- What am I craving, needing, or desiring?

When the emotions have moved, you're free to answer honestly. Instead of focusing on what's expected or what's safe, you're able to get curious about what feels true and aligned with your goals, desires, and values.

Exploration isn't about forcing a decision. You don't have to decide right now. This step is about letting doors open. This is the *"yes, and"* space of innovation, play, and possibility.

Let yourself brainstorm without judgment. Jot down ten, fifteen, twenty wild, interesting, or tiny ideas. Let your imagination stretch beyond the usual. Then choose one that feels worth testing. It doesn't have to be perfect, just your best guess on what to do next.

E is for EXPERIMENT. Once you've explored your options, it's time to choose one and try it. My invitation is for you to do this from a spirit of experimentation rather than pressure. This is about learning through action instead of waiting for certainty. Decide based on values you like, reasons that feel true, or what gives you that internal "yes." Then take the step. Act, implement, and pay attention to what works and what doesn't. Evaluate your experience without shame:

- What worked?
- What didn't?
- What will I try differently next time?

This is how you build momentum. Real change, growth, and learning happens through iterative, aligned action. You don't need a perfect plan. You just need the willingness to experiment, learn, and keep going.

When you allow yourself to feel your emotions and then move through the F.R.E.E. process, you start building a life that is aligned, intentional, and self-led. It's no longer a life that's dictated by old stories, outdated patterns, or fear-based reactions.

You stop living on autopilot and start living on purpose.

Emotional awareness and strategic action are not enemies. They're teammates. First, you stay. Then, you move. First, you feel. Then, you create.

Here's a truth that most people miss. If you're willing to feel *any* emotion, you become unstoppable.

Think about it. What holds most people back isn't the situation itself. It's the emotion they're afraid they'll have to feel. *Embarrassment. Rejection. Disappointment. Guilt. Shame.*

If those feelings didn't scare you, what would you try? What risks would you take? What dreams would you finally pursue?

Maybe you'd...

- Finally ask for the raise.
- Pitch that dream client or launch the business idea that's been gathering dust in your notes app.
- Have the conversation you've been rehearsing in your head for months.
- Book the solo trip that keeps showing up in your daydreams.
- Share your art, your words, or your story... even if no one claps
- Walk away from something that looks "fine" on the outside but feels like slow self-abandonment on the inside.

In Pursuit Insight:
Emotional presence is not weakness. It's wisdom. When there is no feeling you're unwilling to feel, you become unstoppable.

That's the power of emotional willingness. When you stop fearing your own internal experience, the world opens up. You stop arranging your life to avoid discomfort and start building a life that actually reflects who you are and what you want.

Compass Check:
- What emotion have I been resisting lately?
- What do I make it mean about me?
- What permission do I need to offer myself right now?
- Where do I feel this emotion in my body?
- What might happen if I didn't judge this feeling, but sat with it instead?

Safety as a Strategy: Understanding and Regulating Your Nervous System

Most of us try to think our way to calm. We sit there spiraling inside our heads, running scenarios, bargaining with imagined outcomes, trying to outwit the discomfort. *"If I could just figure it out. If I could just control this. If I could just talk myself down."* But no matter how many times you circle the thought, the anxiety doesn't lift, because safety isn't a concept. It's a feeling. And your body, not your brain, is the first place that registers safety or threat.

You can repeat a thousand affirmations, but if your nervous system is in protection mode, no amount of mindset work will override it. The body is the barometer. It doesn't care what you believe intellectually. It cares what it *feels*. And if your nervous system senses danger (whether that danger is a bear in the woods or the emotional risk of being seen), it reacts the same way.

This is why staying with emotions is so hard, especially for high performers. We've spent years training our minds to override discomfort, hustle through the hard stuff, and keep it together no matter what. We are fluent in the language of pushing through. We've built entire identities around being the one who gets it done, holds it all, and doesn't break.

But that kind of wiring, while it may help you succeed on paper, won't help you stay present in your life. It won't help you pursue what matters in a way that actually feels aligned, sustainable, or alive. The kind of pursuit that leads to fulfillment and satisfaction requires a nervous system that can hold the energy of big emotions, big dreams, and big risks. Without this, the pursuit either burns us out or shuts us down.

Creating nervous system safety is what expands our capacity, not just for the hard moments, but for the joy, success, and fulfillment we say we want.

A lot of people unknowingly have a low capacity for success itself. They're not just afraid of failure, they're afraid of what success might bring: visibility, responsibility, judgment, the risk of disappointing others, or the pressure to sustain it. Without the capacity to hold both ends of the spectrum, joy and grief, expansion and contraction, failure and success, we unconsciously self-sabotage or shrink back when life gets bigger than what our system can currently tolerate.

Nervous system work helps widen that window so we can fully receive, experience, and sustain the life we're building.

So, let's talk about what's happening under the surface. Your nervous system is wired to keep you alive. It constantly scans for cues of safety or threat. Every second, without you realizing it, your body is asking, *"Am I safe?"* And the answer to that question determines everything.

When it senses threat, even the subtlest whiff of rejection or risk, it activates your survival system: fight, flight, freeze, or fawn. This is great when you're actually in danger. These are brilliant adaptations. They're your body doing its best to protect you from perceived harm.

But here's where things get messy. Your nervous system doesn't distinguish between real physical danger and the emotional risk of failure, visibility, or vulnerability. The body registers them both as a threat. So, when you're about to launch a project, say something honest, or pursue something that deeply matters to you, your brain might be like, *"Let's go!"* but your body is screaming, *"Absolutely not."*

When that survival system flips on, it hijacks your brain, literally. Your prefrontal cortex, which is the part responsible for big-picture thinking, creativity, and thoughtful decision-making, goes offline. It's like someone unplugged the Wi-Fi. You can't think clearly because your system is too busy scanning for exits.

You default to habituated programming. You procrastinate. You numb out. You snap at your partner. You reach for wine, or your phone, or perfectionism, or people-pleasing. You find yourself doing anything *but* the thing you actually wanted to do. It's important to note that it's not because you don't want to do the thing. It's because your system doesn't feel safe enough to move toward it.

That's why nervous system regulation isn't a luxury. It's not a bonus. It's *the strategy*. It's the difference between being able to show up for your life or constantly getting derailed by emotional landmines.

If your body doesn't perceive safety, you will stall out or sabotage your pursuit, no matter how much your brain wants the outcome.

Building the capacity to regulate your nervous system isn't about becoming some Zen monk or an emotionless robot who never gets stressed. It's about creating enough internal safety that you can move through discomfort, big emotions, big risks, and big visibility, without collapsing or betraying yourself in the process.

That's the work. That's freedom.

So, let's talk about how to build that safety.

The first key is awareness. Most of us are running around completely disconnected from what our bodies are trying to tell us because we've trained ourselves to override it. We hustle through stress. We *"power through"* exhaustion. We ignore the signals until the body finally screams at us (hello migraines, burnout, random rage spirals).

If you want more capacity, it starts with tuning back in.

Start simple. When you feel overwhelmed, anxious, on edge, pause and ask: *Where is this living in my body?* Are your shoulders tense, scrunched up like armor? Is your jaw locked tight? Are your hands curled into fists? Is your stomach in knots?

Your body will tell you. It always tells the truth. You just have to be willing to listen.

Once you notice what's happening, the next step is regulation.

The goal here isn't about forcing yourself to be calm or faking composure so you can be productive again. True regulation is about staying connected to yourself while the discomfort moves through. It's about holding the emotion without collapsing under it.

Regulating your nervous system and allowing emotions through the S.P.A.C.E. method work hand in hand as part of the same process. When you use S.P.A.C.E., you're building the skill of staying present with the raw emotion itself, letting it rise, move, and pass without resistance. Regulation tools help you support your system while you do that work. They don't override or suppress emotion. They create the inner conditions that make it *safe enough* to feel.

When your nervous system is stuck in fight, flight, freeze, or fawn, it's almost impossible to fully allow an emotion because it feels threatening, like something to run from or shut down. Regulation gives you the capacity to stay in S.P.A.C.E. longer and deeper.

And the more you practice S.P.A.C.E., the more your nervous system learns that feeling big emotions is safe. They reinforce each other. You're teaching your system that you can handle hard feelings, and that they will pass. You're cueing your body and brain that there is no emergency, and no need to escape.

This is what builds real capacity over time.

Let's start with breath. It's your most powerful, immediate lever.

Slow, intentional exhales tell your nervous system you're safe. You're not in danger. You can soften now.

This isn't just feel-good fluff, it's biology. A long exhale shifts you out of fight-or-flight and into rest-and-digest. Your breath is the fastest bridge between survival and presence. Use it.

Another underrated tool is orienting and grounding. When you're starting to spiral, pause and look around. Let your eyes slowly move across the space. Find five things you can see. Feel your feet on the floor. Say out loud: *"I'm here. I'm safe. I'm not in danger."* These cues help interrupt the tunnel vision that comes with overwhelm. They anchor you back into the present moment.

Movement is powerful too. Shake out your hands. Stand and stretch. Walk around the block. Let your body move the stress through. Unprocessed survival energy doesn't just evaporate. If you don't give it a way out, it stays stuck. That stuck energy is what turns into shutdown, burnout, or self-sabotage. Move your body and help it process what it's holding.

And please don't underestimate the power of self-talk. Your nervous system is listening.

If you say, *"I can't handle this,"* your body will believe you.
If you say, *"I'm safe. I can feel this. I know how to stay,"* your body hears that, too.

Talk to yourself like you would to someone you love. Use your words to regulate, not to sabotage.

Now, let me be clear, regulation is *not* about perfection. You are not going to reach some magical state where you never get triggered or stressed again. That's called being a robot, not a human.

The goal here is to increase your capacity to stay with yourself when life gets messy, because it *will*.

The more capacity you build, the more resilience you have. And the more resilience you have, the more freedom you have to pursue what matters to you... even when it's hard, even when it's uncertain, even when your brain is throwing all the old fear at you.

Your body will guide you. It will tell you when you're pushing too far, too fast. It will tell you when you need to pause, ground, breathe, or move. It will also tell you when you're ready to expand and take the next big step.

When you learn to listen, you stop fighting yourself. You stop working *against* your system and start working *with* it. And that, my friend, is where real freedom lives.

Emotional regulation isn't about avoiding discomfort. It's about building enough inner safety that you can stay with life—fully present, fully alive, fully capable of holding both the vulnerability of the pursuit *and* the power of your becoming.

Rewiring Emotional Safety: How to Become a Safe Place for Yourself

If you want to stay with hard emotions, regulate your nervous system, and pursue big dreams without abandoning yourself, it's not enough to master the tools. Yes, breathwork matters. Yes, grounding techniques can help. Yes, the S.P.A.C.E. method can hold you steady when the tide rises.

But if the voice in your head is sharp, punishing, and poised to strike the second you feel something vulnerable, none of the tools will stick. The exhale won't land if your nervous system is bracing for impact. The pause won't soothe you if your inner world still feels hostile. The space you create will feel like a trap, not a sanctuary, if the person sitting inside it (yourself) isn't someone you trust.

This is the deeper layer of emotional safety. This is the invisible infrastructure beneath every coping tool and strategy. You have to become a safe place for yourself. This safety can't exist only in theory or as a future goal when external circumstances change. It must begin now. You have to create it in this moment, in the discomfort, in the chaos, and in the weight of emotions you can't quite name.

Most of us weren't taught how to do this. We were taught how to perform. We were taught how to earn love through achievement and how to contort ourselves for approval. We learned to mold ourselves into whatever version made other people most comfortable.

Somewhere along the way, we absorbed messages about which emotions made us lovable and which ones made us too much, too sensitive, too intense, too needy, too angry, or too dramatic. And when those feelings inevitably rose up, we turned on ourselves. We silenced the pain before anyone else had a chance to notice it. We buried the grief before it could inconvenience anyone. We stuffed the rage, disguised the fear, swallowed the shame, and punished ourselves for not being stronger.

"Why are you like this? You should be over this by now. Get it together."

If that's the inner dialogue you're carrying, no amount of external success or nervous system work will give you true freedom, because deep down, your system still doesn't trust you. It doesn't believe you'll stay. It doesn't believe you'll be kind. It doesn't believe you'll offer safety instead of shame.

So, it will continue to trigger protection responses, over and over again, even when the tools are right in front of you.

I remember standing in my kitchen one Tuesday morning, staring at the Google Calendar on my phone like it had personally betrayed me. Back-to-back meetings, a deadline I agreed to (and instantly regretted), and a reminder to *"start workout challenge!!"* blinking at me like some overachieving cheerleader.

And I thought, *What was I thinking?*
Oh right, I wasn't. That was past-me, throwing stuff on the calendar like

future-me was some kind of superhero with no needs, no emotions, and no human limitations.

It wasn't just the overwhelm. It was the realization that I had stopped treating myself like someone I cared about. I was outsourcing my well-being to a version of me I didn't even respect.

That was one of those moments that told me I didn't trust myself, not really.

To be clear, I'm not talking about the kind of trust that says, *"You'll always get it right."* I mean the kind of trust that says, *"Even if it goes sideways, I've still got you."* The kind that says, *"You're allowed to mess up, and I won't weaponize it against you."*

This is where emotional safety begins. It doesn't start with breathing exercises or journaling prompts (although I love both). It starts with self-trust. It starts with the relationship you have with yourself when the pressure's on, when the results don't come, and when you miss the mark.

If you're still dragging your past self through the mud for what they didn't know, how can your current self ever feel safe enough to take a leap? If you believe your future self is just waiting to say, *"Told you so,"* why would you risk going after something big, bold, or vulnerable?

You wouldn't. You'd shrink. You'd stall. You'd stay small. You'd hide and limit yourself to avoid the future shaming.

Rewiring emotional safety means creating a different internal dynamic. One where your past self is honored for doing the best they could. One where your future self is a soft place to land, not another critic to outrun.

Imagine what would shift if you truly believed your future self would meet you with love, even if it didn't work out. What would you go after if you knew that no matter the outcome, you wouldn't beat yourself up for it later?

And while we're at it, let's stop setting up future-you to suffer. You know the move: *"Sure, I'll commit to that thing I don't want to do because I'll figure it out later."* That's not time management. That's betrayal. And when you do it enough times, your nervous system stops trusting you. No wonder you feel burnt out.

True self-trust is built in those tiny moments when you say, *"I hear you, and I've got you."* You create emotional safety when you don't override your limits or silence your needs. You build trust with yourself when you set a boundary, not to look powerful, but because it honors your peace.

That's what builds integrity. That's what creates safety.

And here's the magic. When your system knows you won't shame your past, abandon your present, or dump all your problems on your future self, you start to move with a different kind of freedom. You stop micromanaging your every move. You stop using achievement to outrun judgment. You stop performing.

And you start being a messy, brilliant, ambitious... human.

You start going after your wildest dreams, because now, finally, it feels safe to try.

In Pursuit Insight:
If you can trust yourself to have your own back, past, present, and future, there is nothing you won't be brave enough to try.

The truth is that living a bigger life will always require you to hold more. It will ask you to hold more joy, but also more uncertainty, more exposure, more emotional depth, more potential, more failure, and more success. You cannot expand into that kind of life without first expanding your internal sense of safety.

This kind of emotional safety is not just a nice idea. It is a skill, and it is one you can start practicing today.

It begins in the moment when that old, familiar voice rises up and says, *"You always mess this up,"* and you choose to respond in a new way. You meet yourself with something kinder and more honest. You offer a response that encourages who you are becoming and supports the direction you are heading.

It might sound like, *"Of course this feels hard. Of course, this hurts. I am still here."*

When you talk to yourself like that, something powerful happens. You stop treating discomfort like a problem to solve and start seeing it as part of the process. You quit chasing perfection as proof of your worth and start anchoring into compassion instead. You remind yourself it's okay to not have all the answers. You communicate to yourself that it's okay to feel messy, uncertain, and real. It's okay to be wildly, beautifully human.

Each time you do this, your nervous system releases just a little bit more tension. Your capacity increases. You begin to replace a culture of internal perfectionism with a culture of internal permission. The more consistently you meet yourself in this way, the more your system will believe you.

Over time, your body learns that intense emotions are not dangerous. To be clear, this doesn't happen because they feel easy, but because you have proven that you will not abandon yourself when they arise.

This is what builds emotional capacity. And emotional capacity is what allows you to live a fuller life.

If you are unable to sit with the shame of being seen, you will find ways to avoid visibility. If you cannot tolerate the fear of disappointing others, you will shrink your boundaries and water down your dreams. If you cannot hold the vulnerability that comes with success, you will unconsciously sabotage it.

Emotional safety is not something that shows up once you are successful.

It is what makes success possible, and sustainable, in the first place.

When you become a safe place for yourself, you stop outsourcing that safety to others. You stop living under the weight of external validation or internal criticism. You step into self-leadership.

And self-leadership means you take responsibility for the emotional environment you live in every day.

You stop waiting for someone else to make you feel safe, worthy, or enough.

You begin to understand that only *you* can do that for yourself.

One of the tools you already have is the S.T.E.A.R. model. You can use it to choose, with intention, the thoughts that generate the emotional state you want to lead from.

The stories you tell yourself about who you are and what you are capable of directly shape your experience of safety, worthiness, and enough-ness. Those internal narratives fuel your emotions. Your emotions then drive your actions, and your actions create your outcomes.

When you generate safety from within, you stop waiting to feel ready, and start trusting yourself to move.

That becomes the foundation for every bold thing you want to create.

When your system knows it is safe to feel, safe to expand, safe to pursue, safe to fail, and safe to succeed, you stop holding back.

You become someone who leads themself. And that kind of self-leadership is unstoppable.

Compass Check:
- What kind of relationship do I want to have with my past, present, and future self?
- If I fully trusted myself to have my own back, what would I give myself permission to pursue right now?
- What story am I currently telling myself about who I am, what's possible for me, and what I'm capable of?
- Are the thoughts I'm thinking creating the emotional state I want to lead from, or keeping me stuck?
- What is one thought I can choose on purpose this week to fuel self-trust and forward momentum?

Chapter 7:

STRUCTURE the Support

Boundaries as Love: Build a Life That Supports You Back

You're not meant to carry it all alone.

Read that again. This time, don't just skim it with your eyes. Feel it with your whole body. Let it drop below the shoulders you've taught to stay squared, the jaw you've learned to clench, and the spine you've held straight even when your soul is buckling. Let that sentence land right where the pressure lives. Let it speak to the part of you that shows up strong for everyone else but quietly longs for someone to show up for you. Let it touch the part that never asks for help but desperately wants to exhale.

What I'm offering here might be hard to receive, because many of us have mistaken self-sufficiency for strength. We've conflated over-functioning with leadership. Somewhere along the road of being reliable, responsible, and relentless, we started believing the lie that carrying it all alone is a badge of honor. We've told ourselves that independence is nobility and that being able to handle everything on our own is proof of our worth and safety.

I see you. I also see how this story, beautiful and well-intentioned as it is, eventually breaks people. It creates leaders who look polished on the outside and empty on the inside. It builds businesses, careers, and lives that the person living them secretly doesn't want anymore. It generates success that doesn't feel safe to hold because the person has no scaffolding under them, no true support system.

I've sat across from too many brilliant, successful people with eyes full of exhaustion and hearts full of quiet weariness to believe the lie anymore. I've watched the most capable humans collapse under the weight of a life they built but no longer want to hold. I've watched clients whisper through tears, *"I don't know how to keep going like this,"* just moments after being praised on a podcast or applauded at an awards ceremony.

What I've seen too many times to count is that self-sufficiency, when worshipped as identity, becomes a prison.

It's not just that it's lonely.

It's that it's unsustainable.

No one does big things alone.

Perhaps more importantly, no one sustains big things alone.

That doesn't make you weak. That makes you wise. It means you're waking up to the truth that your pursuit needs a support system. That's not a concession or surrender. It's actually strategy and leadership.

One of my favorite metaphors for this came from a yoga class I took years ago. After an intense flow, the instructor guided us through a series of partner stretches.

Now, for context, I'm the type of person who prefers solo workouts, earphones in, don't talk to me. The idea of pairing off with a stranger, touching each other, and physically coordinating a stretch wasn't exactly my dream scenario. But I complied, begrudgingly, and what I discovered surprised me.

There were muscles I couldn't access on my own. Positions I'd tried a hundred times solo suddenly released under the tension and counterbalance of another person's presence. There were parts of me I simply couldn't access without a different kind of support.

That moment never left me because life, like yoga, has places you can't stretch into alone.

Some breakthroughs—emotional, professional, spiritual—require a counterweight, a mirror, or a hand on your back reminding you it's okay to lean. You weren't designed to do this by yourself.

I tell clients all the time, *"The photo can't see the frame."* You may be sharp, intuitive, wildly competent, and still have blind spots. In fact, the more high-functioning you are, the more likely it is you've overdeveloped certain muscles and neglected others.

You've learned to run hard and think fast, but sometimes the thing you most need is someone who can see what you can't when your head is down. This is where a mentor, a coach, a trusted peer, or a partner comes in handy. They can hold a wider view when your lens narrows. They can say, *"I see where this is going. Let's slow down. Let's reroute. Let's stretch in a new direction."*

They bring a vantage point you simply can't access from inside your own head.

It's like having a traffic helicopter or GPS app that can see the whole map, not just the road you're driving on. When you're barreling forward, focused on doing all the things, they can spot the traffic jams or detours ahead and say, *"Hey, take the off-ramp here,"* or *"Shift lanes."*

It's the structure and support that helps you get there faster and with less stress. The right people can reflect what you can't see yet. They can help you stretch into a capacity you didn't know you had. They can help you build the strength to hold more success, joy, and aligned action, without burning out.

And I want to be clear. This isn't cheating or cutting corners. This is what smart, efficient, and effective people do. They use every tool, every perspective, and every ounce of support available to make the pursuit more sustainable and more effective. But here's the catch. You have to build this support system with intention. And one tool for that is *boundaries*.

Boundaries aren't walls. They aren't barbed wire fences or passive-aggressive ultimatums. Boundaries are not about locking people out. They're about letting the right people in.

They are the emotional scaffolding that supports your pursuit. Without them, you'll take on too much, get drained by unsupportive relationships, or sabotage your own goals because you're trying to do it all from a place of depletion. Boundaries are love in action.

One of my favorite quotes on boundaries comes from Prentis Hemphill who said, *"Boundaries are the distance at which I can love you and me simultaneously."*

Boundaries communicate that you respect yourself enough to honor what you need to stay resourced, present, and fully engaged in your pursuit. They also indicate that you trust others enough to allow them to support you where it makes sense, and that you trust them enough to handle your truth.

This is not about becoming hyper-defended or controlling your environment to the point of isolation. It's about creating clarity around where your energy goes, what relationships feed it, and where you can delegate or receive help to expand your capacity.

This includes your clients, your colleagues, your family, your partner, your calendar, your inbox, and your self-talk. Every one of them has a relationship to your boundaries, or lack thereof.

Interestingly, the same people who struggle to set boundaries also tend to struggle to receive support. At their core, both require believing you're worthy of being protected, prioritized, and poured into.

Setting boundaries is one way we honor that belief. Receiving support is another. Both are essential if you want to sustain what you're building. High-achieving folks are often exceptional at *giving* support, but not so great at *receiving* it.

Somewhere along the way, we internalized the belief that asking for help makes us a burden. We decided that delegating is risky. That no one will do it as well as we can. (How many of you just laughed out loud thinking, *"Is this woman reading my mind?!"*) So we keep proving our strength by carrying what's crushing us.

You know the voice. It sounds like, *"It's faster if I just do it myself."*

Or, *"I don't want to bother them."*

Or, *"If I ask for help, they'll think I can't handle it."*

The irony is that while we fear appearing weak, we're weakening our own pursuit by refusing to structure it with support.

Here's a reframe I want to offer you. Refusing support isn't strength. It's self-sabotage. If you're serious about building a life that feels as good as it looks, one where you're not constantly teetering on the edge of burnout while smiling for the camera, then support is not optional. It's essential.

In Pursuit Insight:
You can't create an aligned, fully alive life by running yourself into the ground. Sustainable pursuit requires structure: boundaries that protect you, rhythms that resource you, and rituals that reconnect you to what matters most.

That includes building boundaries around your time, energy, priorities, and capacity. What will you, and won't you, give your energy to? Where are you willing to receive help instead of performing superhuman?

If you're trying to run a business, raise a family, manage your health, nurture your relationships, evolve your emotional world, *and* still somehow vacuum the house and answer every text without any structural support, you're not being strategic.

You're drowning. You've become the bottleneck in your own life. Full stop. You will burn out. And when you do, the very pursuit you care about will suffer.

Your capacity is not fixed. It's something you can grow, but only if you are willing to stop defaulting to doing it all for everyone, all the time.

It expands when you stop wasting energy on things that don't align with your pursuit.

This includes over-functioning, over-explaining, and overcommitting.

It also includes letting go of guilt-driven yeses and resentment-fueled obligations, as well as pretending you're fine when you're not.

One of the highest forms of self-leadership is learning where your line is and having the courage to honor it.

That means learning to make requests instead of silent assumptions. It means communicating expectations instead of hoping people just *know*. It means stating consequences, not to punish others, but to honor yourself. It also means setting boundaries *with yourself*, with the version of you who wants to say yes to everything so you don't disappoint anyone.

Keep in mind that every yes out of alignment is a no to the life you're trying to build.

Let me give you an example.

A client of mine, a brilliant business owner and mother of three, came to me completely fried. She was saying yes to every PTA request, every client ask, every late-night favor, every family obligation. She told herself she was being generous, selfless, and helpful.

But underneath it all, she was actually afraid. Afraid of being seen as selfish. Afraid of letting people down. Afraid of not being liked.

Every yes she gave to protect her image was robbing time, energy, and mental space from the business and life she was trying to build. Her vision didn't lack clarity. It lacked *protection*.

She wasn't running out of capacity because she wasn't capable. She was running out of capacity because she was bleeding energy in a hundred directions that weren't aligned with her pursuit. So, we worked on getting clear about what was truly in alignment, and then setting boundaries both with others and with herself.

That meant saying: *"Here's what I can do. Here's what I can't. Here's what I need in order to stay resourced, and here's how I'm going to hold that line."*

She also got clear about the patterns that were burning her out:

No more saying yes out of guilt.
No more filling her calendar to prove her worth.
No more pretending she could carry it all without consequence.

And guess what? The sky didn't fall. Some people were uncomfortable. Some adjusted, and some didn't. But she reclaimed her time, her energy, her voice, and her vision.

That's the power of boundaries. They're not meant to shut people out or dole out punishments. They are a tool to help you build a life that actually *fits*. They're not harsh or selfish. They are sacred.

The life you're building deserves a foundation strong enough to hold it.

Compass Check:

As you move through this chapter, consider the following questions:

- Where am I trying to hold everything myself?
- Where do I need to set or strengthen boundaries to protect my energy and time?
- Where am I resisting support that could actually expand my capacity?
- What relationships, mentors, or resources could I invite in to help me pursue what matters most?

Stop Back-Burnering Your Needs: Calendar Mastery and Energy Audit

If you want to know what you're actually prioritizing, don't look at your vision board. Look at your calendar. Look at the days, weeks, and months that make up your real life. Which ones leave you breathless, bitter, stretched thin, or strangely numb? Which ones leave you grounded, fulfilled, and lit up? The calendar tells the truth. It's not going to show you the version of the life you fantasize about in the shower. It's going to show you the one you're actually living in. Is it filled with meetings you dread, errands you didn't want to agree to, and commitments that you keep mostly because guilt speaks louder than your gut? Or is it anchored with things that reflect your values, feed your energy, and move you closer to the life you say you want?

Here's what I see all the time. People tell me they want a more alive, aligned, purpose-filled life. But when we pull up their calendar, it's packed with everything *but* that. There's no room to breathe. No space to think. The very things that would nourish their pursuit, rest, joy, creativity, movement, stillness, relationship, soul-time, are shoved to the margins like an afterthought. Or worse, they're not even on the page. It's no wonder why they're exhausted and disconnected from what once lit them up. It starts to make sense why they feel empty even though they think they should be grateful.

Let me say this clearly. If you are constantly back-burnering your needs and values in service of everyone else's priorities, you are building a life that guarantees burnout. You are not a victim of your calendar. You are its creator. And as I said before, every *"yes"* you say when you mean *"no"* is a vote for a life you don't actually want.

I know that might sting a little. It stung for me too the first time I realized I was performing obligation instead of living alignment. But that sting is also an invitation. It's a wake-up call that says, *if you created it, you have the power to recreate it, on purpose and on your terms.*

I used to think calendar planning was just for Type A overachievers who loved color-coded spreadsheets and living in 15-minute increments, but then I realized something. My schedule wasn't just a list of appointments. It was a reflection of my values. Or at least, it was supposed to be. Instead, it had become a junk drawer of everyone else's priorities. It was filled with meetings I didn't want to be in, events I didn't remember saying yes to, and obligations I was quietly resenting.

That's when Calendar Mastery clicked. And no, it's not just another *"productivity hack"* someone on the internet cooked up to help you squeeze more into your already overflowing day. This is different. Calendar Mastery is an act of radical self-respect. It's how you take your power back from the chaos and start building a schedule that actually honors the life you say you want.

It means putting the big rocks in first. This includes things like your health, your peace, your family dinner, and your freaking joy. It means blocking white space into your days to breathe, think, and remember who you are. And listen, I get it. You might feel guilty even thinking about this. That voice might pop up saying, *"Who do you think you are to prioritize yourself?"* But here's the mindset shift I want to hand you right now: *It's not selfish. It's leadership.*

Every time you shove yourself to the back burner, you're not just burning out. You're teaching everyone around you that your needs are optional. You're modeling self-abandonment instead of self-leadership. And eventually, that will cost you everything that matters to you, like your energy, your purpose, and your passion. This isn't about getting more done. This is about becoming the kind of person who protects what matters most.

Let's connect this to the S.T.E.A.R. model that you learned earlier in this book. Remember, every action you take is fueled by an emotion, and every emotion is fueled by a thought. So, if you sit down to do this work thinking, *"This is a waste of time,"* or *"I shouldn't need to block time for myself,"* or *"It's easier if I just keep going,"* then what kind of action will follow?

Exactly. You'll either avoid the process entirely or approach it through the lens of guilt, which only leads to half-hearted effort and unsustainable results. That is not the energy that fuels a sustainable pursuit. You can't white-knuckle your way into a meaningful life. You've got to build the kind of inner world where doing what's right for you doesn't feel like breaking the rules. It feels like coming home.

Here's what that shift might look like in practice:

Example 1:

- Thought: I am the CEO of my time and energy.
- Emotion: Empowered
- Action: Proactively audit my calendar, remove what's misaligned, and block space for my priorities.

Example 2:

- Thought: Honoring my needs is what allows me to show up at my highest level.
- Emotion: Committed
- Action: Block time for rest, creative work, and relationships before adding external requests.

Example 3:

- Thought: Every yes I say to someone else is also a yes or no to myself.
- Emotion: Thoughtful
- Action: Pause before committing and make decisions about commitments and what I put on my calendar with clarity and sovereignty.

As you move into this work, I want you to pause and ask, *What thoughts and emotions will best support me in taking aligned, self-honoring action with my calendar and my commitments?* Generate those first, on purpose. Lasting, sustainable change doesn't come through gritted teeth and a hustle-and-grind mentality. The pursuit you want is built from the inside out and executed through belief-fueled action. That's how you make it stick.

So how do you begin? One of my favorite practices to give clients is something I call the Calendar Energy Audit. It's simple, sobering, and clarifying.

Start by pulling up the next two weeks of your calendar and ask yourself:

- What is here because it's aligned with my pursuit and values?
- What is here because of guilt, obligation, or people-pleasing?
- What is draining me that I need to release or renegotiate?
- Where am I scheduling from integrity and self-respect, and where am I scheduling from fear or martyrdom?

This is an invitation to tell yourself the truth, not to judge yourself for it. That's where real change starts.

When you see your time on paper like this, it gets real, fast. The patterns become impossible to unsee. You start to notice how often you say *"yes"* and leave it for your future self to handle, hoping they'll be more rested or less overwhelmed by then. You catch yourself clinging to the unrealistic hope that your future self will magically have the energy, clarity, and bandwidth you already know you don't have today.

If something doesn't feel like it's worth your time today, it's not going to feel worth your time next Monday either. Stop putting stuff on the calendar like future you is your personal assistant. Your future self is you, with the same needs, limits, and heart. Start making decisions today like your energy is sacred, because it is.

Calendar Mastery also means setting boundaries in advance. If you know you need two nights a week to chill, create, recharge, or just stare at the ceiling in silence, BLOCK. THEM. OFF. before the invites and *"quick favors"* start rolling in.

If you know you're creating something important (a project, a shift, a life), don't just hope for time, schedule it and protect it.

If physical or emotional health matters (and it absolutely should, in my humble opinion), don't just squeeze it in after everything else. Schedule it in. It goes first. Period.

And here's what starts to happen when you do this:

The resentment begins to lift.
The creativity starts to return.
The tightness in your chest when Sunday night rolls around begins to ease.
You stop feeling like you're chasing your life and start feeling like you're living it.
You stop living in reaction mode and start leading with intention.
You shift from being stretched in every direction to standing rooted in what matters.

Instead of constantly pushing your needs aside, you begin honoring them as the fuel that powers your best work and your most present self. You remember that your pursuit doesn't need you to be everything to everyone. It requires you to be resourced, steady, and aligned to *you*. It asks you to come home to who you are. That starts right here, with the courage to lead your time like your life depends on it. Because it does.

Compass Check:
- What thoughts about my time, energy, and worth will best support the life I'm in pursuit of?
- What emotions do I want to generate that will fuel empowered, self-honoring action with my calendar?
- Am I currently choosing thoughts that create those emotions or ones that keep me stuck in guilt, resentment, or performance?
- What is one new thought I can practice this week that will help me lead my time, not react to it?

Rituals & Rhythms for Self-Leadership: Build the Support System Your Pursuit Needs

When I trained for my marathon, I had to let go of a lot of what I thought I knew about progress. Like most high achievers, I was conditioned to go hard, push through, and always do more. My brain fed off the hustle. It loved the thrill of stacking accomplishments and the pride of carrying everything without breaking.

But marathon training doesn't reward that kind of constant output. It punishes it. You can't run your hardest every day and expect to get stronger. That's not a training plan. That's a breakdown plan. If you try to muscle through without recovery, you will end up exhausted, burned out, or giving up. This doesn't happen because you didn't want it badly enough. It happens because your body cannot sustain output without restoration. Ask any seasoned marathoner. They'll tell you it's not the race day that makes you, it's the rhythm leading up to it.

The training schedule is intentionally designed: long runs, slow recovery jogs, cross-training, rest days, taper weeks. Each one has a role to play. Every element has a purpose. None of it is extra. None of it is indulgent. It's the structure that makes the goal possible. Without it, the finish line stays out of reach. Or worse, you crawl across it wrecked and wondering why the victory doesn't feel worth it.

That lesson stayed with me far beyond the race, because the pursuit of your goals and dreams works the same way. You need more than just intensity. You need rituals and rhythms that expand your capacity so you can sustain the effort your pursuit requires. You need a support system that isn't just made up of people, but also anchored in your practices, your habits, and your internal leadership. Without it, you won't last. Intensity without rhythm doesn't lead to greatness. It leads to burnout, resentment, and eventually, disconnection from the very life you're trying to build.

I see it all the time. Clients with big dreams and even bigger ambition try to sprint their way through a marathon. They pour everything into the goal but forget to pour back into themselves. Then they wonder why the fire they started with fizzles out halfway through. It's like trying to power a road trip with nothing but adrenaline and epic playlists. You can blast your music, keep the windows down, and ride the high for a while, but if you never stop for gas, you're not going to make it. The car doesn't care how motivated you are. It needs fuel. It needs maintenance. It needs rest stops. So do you.

Rituals and rhythms aren't just feel-good extras. They are your internal infrastructure. They are how you regulate your nervous system, renew your energy, reconnect to your vision, and stay resourced for the long game. Without them, you stay stuck in reactive mode. You chase the next goal, put out the next fire, and slowly lose touch with yourself in the process. But when you lead yourself with rhythm and intention, everything changes. You stop surviving your pursuit and start living it.

This part is important, so pay attention. This is not about adding another list of "*shoulds*" to your plate. You don't need a 5 a.m. miracle morning or a hyper-optimized life that makes you feel like a robot. You don't need 37 new habits or a productivity spreadsheet that micromanages your every breath.

You need a few sacred, intentional practices that anchor you and remind you who you are and what matters. You need practices, rituals, and routines that keep your nervous system in the zone of safety and your mind rooted in truth. These are the things that build trust with yourself. These are the things that let you hold more without collapsing under the weight.

This might look like a Sunday calendar review ritual. The intention here is to create a moment of reconnection where you align your upcoming week with your values so that you don't just plug in obligations. Pause before the week begins and ask yourself, "*What will nourish me? What will drain me? What gets to stay? What needs to go?*" How you lead your time is how you lead your life.

It might look like a daily nervous system regulation practice. This doesn't have to be anything complicated or fancy, just something that brings you back to center. Maybe it's breathwork, a slow walk around the block, or a few minutes of stretching. Or maybe a hot second of stillness might do the trick. Try taking a moment to scan your body and ask, "*What do I need right now?*" It's less about the method and more about the attention. Your body is always speaking. Rituals are how you listen and begin to understand what your body and nervous system are communicating.

You might also try a weekly reflection where you check in with your pursuit. Take a few moments of honest inventory and ask, "*Am I still in alignment with what I say I want? What am I proud of? What felt good this week? What felt heavy? What do I need to recalibrate?*" Progress without pause becomes pressure. Reflection is the rhythm that allows growth to become transformation.

A gratitude ritual might sound simple, even cliché, but it's neuroscience-backed magic. What you focus on expands. The practice of naming what's good shifts your entire emotional baseline. It helps you train your mind to look for sufficiency instead of scarcity. It sharpens your attention toward what's working, what's blooming, and what's beautiful right now.

Then there's thought work. This is one of the most powerful rituals I've built into my life. This isn't about fixing your thoughts. It's about getting curious. Sit down daily or weekly and do a thought download where you free-write, no editing, and eavesdrop on your own brain. Get it all out. Write out all the fears, drama, hope, and mental messiness. Then run an Unintentional S.T.E.A.R. model to see how those thoughts are shaping your results. From there, you get to decide: *What thought would serve me better? What emotion do I want to fuel my next action?* That's what it means to lead your mind instead of being led by it.

If you haven't already gotten your copy of the Unblocked Journal, grab it now for prompts and space to practice this. Scan the QR code or go to jessicasmarrocoaching.com/unblocked-journal. This is the work that changes your life.

We can't talk about sacred practices without talking about joy. In a culture that glorifies grit and grind, joy is often treated like a luxury. But joy is fuel. Whether it's a dance break, a creative outlet, a quiet walk, or a belly laugh with someone you love, joy is not extra. It is essential. When you build it into your rhythms, your entire pursuit of success, goals, and dreams becomes lighter, more alive, and more you.

Here's why this matters so much. When you are chasing something big (your healing, your calling, your dream) you will face resistance. You will meet the voice that says, *"Why bother?"* You'll hit emotional lows, doubt storms, and days where you just don't want to keep going. If you don't have rhythms that bring you back to center, you'll start living in reaction mode. You'll self-sabotage. You'll confuse burnout with failure.

Think back to that marathon. No runner shows up to race day having sprinted every training session and skipped their rest days. That would be insane. Yet we do it in our lives all the time. We try to "earn" the breakthrough without honoring the body, the breath, the boundaries that make it sustainable.

The bigger the vision, the more support you need, not less. That includes emotional support, yes. But also, structural support. The invisible scaffolding of rituals that keep you standing when things shake. Self-leadership means you choose to build the system your pursuit needs before you hit the wall. You don't wait for the breakdown. You set the structure now.

It means you decide (intentionally, consistently) that your nervous system matters. Your joy matters. Your ability to recover, reconnect, and renew matters. You treat those things like fuel, not rewards. You ritualize what resources you.

In a pursuit-driven life, the goal is not to do more, faster. It is to go further, fuller, and more faithfully aligned to who you truly are. You get to build a life that supports you back. You can't do that without intentionality, the proper mindset, and rituals and routines to support it. You can't do that if you're constantly burning down your own capacity in the name of "getting ahead." You get to become the kind of person who builds the support system your pursuit needs. And that starts right now with what you choose to ritualize, protect, and honor in your own life.

You do that with small daily choices that become a way of being. These rituals remind you that you are not here to *survive* your dream. You are here to live it fully, deeply, and well.

Compass Check:
- What rituals or rhythms do I already have that support my energy, focus, and pursuit?
- Where am I currently running on hustle instead of sustainability?
- What is one ritual I can add or recommit to this week that will help me lead my time, mind, or body with more intention?
- How can I use gratitude and thought work to align my mindset with the pursuit I want to create?
- What would it look like to treat joy as fuel, not an afterthought?

Chapter 8:

SIMPLIFY the Actions

Aligned Pursuit: Clarify What You Want and Plan Boldly

If you want to take bold action, you have to know where you're aiming. It sounds obvious, almost insultingly simple, but you would be shocked how many people are running full speed toward a destination they never consciously chose. These are the people who know how to hustle, grind, and get results. They're masters at building momentum, but momentum without alignment is a recipe for burnout.

I see it all the time. People pour time, energy, and creativity into goals they don't actually want. Or they chase a watered-down version of a dream because it feels safer, more reasonable, or less likely to be judged. Then they come to me and say, *"I'm doing all the right things. Why does it still feel so unfulfilling?"*

The answer is that it's not just about what you're doing. It's about whether what you're doing is in alignment with what you truly want.

You can build an impressive life and still feel disconnected from it. You can stack achievements and still feel empty. This is the part most people miss.

The first step in simplifying your actions is clarifying your aim. You have to name what you're actually pursuing, and that pursuit has to be true to you. It can't be something that simply checks a box, earns applause, or looks good on paper. It has to be what you deeply, undeniably desire.

This is why I teach clients to ruthlessly clarify and align before they ever map out a strategy. We are not here for performative action. We are not here to build a life that looks good from the outside but feels hollow inside.

We're here for aligned pursuit. That means action that reflects your values, honors your truth, and supports the kind of life you want to live in, not escape from.

If you're not exactly sure what you want, not to worry. I have some questions to help you access your true desire. Grab your journal or notes app on your phone and your hydration of choice. Settle in and give yourself some spaciousness to consider the following questions.

1. What do you want? Like, *really* want? Not what you think is realistic, not what others expect of you. If you get stuck on question one, ask yourself the following questions. If you had one year to live:
    *   What would you STOP doing?
    *   What would you START doing?
    *   What would you NO LONGER care about?
    *   What would you care MORE about?
2. Why do you want it? What about this goal actually matters to you? What will achieving this goal give you? Why does that matter?
3. How do you want to feel in the process of pursuing it?
4. How do you want to feel when you achieve it?

If you're reading those questions and thinking, *"I don't know what I want…"* let me tell you what's likely going on.

When most people say that, it's not because they lack desire. It's because they're already filtering their ideas through *how. How would I make that happen? Could I really pull it off? Is it realistic? What would people think? What if I fail?*

That noise shuts down dreaming before it even starts. For the high achievers in the audience, this happens fast, because if they can't see a path to guaranteed success, they won't even let themselves want it.

Here's how to interrupt that pattern. Separate the process of dreaming from the process of deciding.

Step one is ideation. This is where you get to want what you want. No *how*. No judgment. No filtering. No limits. You're not allowed to kill off ideas here just because you can't yet see how they'd work. This is where you play, imagine, and expand. *"Wouldn't it be cool if..."* energy is welcome here. You are not building a plan in this phase. You are listening to your own longings.

Only after that comes step two, which is discernment. This is the step where you choose and decide. Once you've given yourself permission to dream fully and your desires have been safely expressed, you can move into grounded alignment. Here's where you get real. *What's most aligned right now? What season am I in? What resources do I have? What do I want to make room for?*

You cannot skip straight to step two. If you try to combine these two phases, you'll block yourself. If you try to problem-solve too soon, you'll never surface the truth.

So, if your brain starts spiraling in *"I don't know what I want,"* ask yourself this: *Am I trying to solve the how before I've let myself want?* You can't plan a pursuit you won't allow yourself to name. You have to dream first. You have to give yourself permission to want.

Once you've named what you actually want, and your real desire finally has space to breathe, there's a really good chance your brain will go into full-blown freakout. The second you admit the truth of your pursuit, your survival system chimes in with all its greatest hits:

This is too risky.
You don't know how.
You're not qualified.
It's unrealistic.
What if you fail?
What will people say?

This is not a problem. This is biology. Your brain is trying to protect you from risk, rejection, and the unknown. It's doing its job. But your job is different.

Your job isn't to eliminate those thoughts. It's to expect them, and refuse to believe them or let them run the show.

This is why I have clients write down every single objection their brain throws up when they imagine pursuing their goal. I have them write out every *"What if I fail,"* every *"This is too expensive,"* every *"I've never done this before."* No judgment. No edits. Just get it all out.

Here's where the magic happens. Those objections aren't just noise. They're a map. When you capture them, you can start to neutralize them. You can turn them into action. You turn the fear into fuel by translating each one into what I call *Pursuit Steps*. These are the specific, doable moves that bridge the gap between fear and forward motion.

A Pursuit Step is a concrete, actionable next step that addresses the obstacle. Here are some possible examples.

If your brain says, *"I don't know how to launch a podcast,"* **Your Pursuit Steps are:**

- Research podcast hosting platforms
- Book a 30-minute call with someone who has launched a podcast

If your brain says, *"I'm not good at selling,"* **Your Pursuit Steps are:**

- Learn how to sell by reading one article or taking one course on ethical selling

If your brain says, *"I want to start dating, but I'm afraid I'll get hurt,"* **Your Pursuit Steps are:**

- Make a list of five ways to meet new people
- Sign up for one dating app and message three people
- Tell two trusted friends you're open to being set up
- Practice the skill of creating emotional safety

If your brain says, *"I want to be less critical of myself and others, but that's just how I think,"* **Your Pursuit Steps are:**

- Start a daily thought download to notice critical thoughts
- Reframe one self-critical or judgmental thought each day
- Complete one Compassion Expansion exercise daily to build new thought patterns

If your brain says, *"I'm afraid of being visible,"* **Your Pursuit Steps are:**

- Speak up and share one idea each week during your team huddle

- Do one live video or post one vulnerable story to practice showing up

See how that works? We don't fight the thoughts. We partner with them. We let them reveal what's needed. From there, we build action by taking one Pursuit Step at a time.

This is what planning boldly really looks like. You don't need a perfect master plan to take bold action. You need clarity on what you want, awareness of the thoughts and obstacles coming up, and a list of small, actionable Pursuit Steps that move you forward one step at a time.

You do not need to know the whole path to start moving. You do not need to have all the answers, all the qualifications, or some magical green light from the universe. Bold action is not about certainty, it's about willingness.

It's like taking a road trip from New York to California. You don't wait in your driveway until you can see the Pacific Ocean. You start driving. You trust that the next road sign, the next turn, and the next city will reveal itself once you're in motion. The same is true for your pursuit

You do not need to have the entire master plan. You just need to start. Name what you want. Write down your fears. Turn those fears into small, doable actions. Then get moving. That's how the path unfolds. It doesn't happen all at once. It happens one decision, one stretch of road, one brave, imperfect move at a time.

This is your official invitation.

1. Clarify what you truly want.
2. Write down every objection and obstacle your brain offers.
3. Turn those obstacles into Pursuit Steps - small, doable next steps.
4. Commit to walking the path before you can see the entire map.

Then it happens. You finally start taking action steps and *bam*, you slam into another wall, the fear of being a beginner.

This one is brutal, especially for high performers who've grown accustomed to being the best in the room. Going after something you've never pursued before means shedding the armor of expertise. It means being seen trying, fumbling, and learning.

Here's the thing, You don't get to the 100th iteration without the first. The messy crumb layer on the cake is required to get the aesthetically pleasing top layer.

Listen, I don't make the rules, but you don't become excellent without starting as a beginner. You don't create mastery by avoiding the messy first steps. If you demand perfection or competence out of the gate, you'll paralyze yourself. You'll avoid action entirely to protect your ego. When that happens, your pursuit stalls out. This doesn't happen because you aren't capable. It happens simply because you're unwilling to be seen trying.

Being a beginner is not a failure. It's a flex. It is the ultimate sign of strength. It means you're growing. It means you're building capacity for the life you actually want. It means you're brave enough to choose action over ego.

Consider this. All the people you admire—the athletes, authors, speakers, entrepreneurs, leaders—they were all beginners once. They were willing to take the first step, get messy, and iterate. You can't skip this part, and the more you normalize that discomfort, the faster you move through it.

In Pursuit Insight: Remember this when your brain tries to talk you out of starting. Everyone who is where you want to be has been where you are right now.

So let your first attempt be messy. Let your first move be small. Let your first draft be imperfect. Most pursuits worth having begin with a step that feels too small and a heart that feels unsure.

As you take your next Pursuit Step, remind yourself that there is no shame in being new. There is only courage in showing up. The life you want isn't built by waiting until you feel *ready*. It's built by getting in motion, staying in motion, and letting each bold action teach you what's next.

Messy Action, Massive Progress: How to Actually Move Forward

Okay. So now you know what you want. You've named the dream. You've mapped the Pursuit Steps. You've even started shifting the way you think about taking action.

This is the moment where things get real. It's also the place where most people slam on the brakes.

This doesn't happen because you're lazy or don't care. You *do*, in fact, care, and you're probably quite willing to work really hard for what you want. But the moment action becomes real, the mind starts screaming for certainty. It wants guarantees, step-by-step instructions, and a crystal ball.

Suddenly, you're overthinking every move, obsessing about the "right" or most efficient way to do it, and convincing yourself that you need a perfect plan before you start.

You tell yourself you'll move forward *when you feel ready, when it feels safe*, or *when it all makes sense*. But waiting for perfect conditions is the fastest way to stay stuck. This can result in weeks, months, or sometimes years going by with your dreams and goals on hold.

Here's your loving interruption. You do not create massive progress through perfect planning. You create it through messy, iterative, learning-driven action. You create it by being willing to move, even when (ahem, *especially* when) the path is foggy.

One of my favorite tools for this is something I call the **D.I.L.I. Method: Decide. Implement. Learn. Iterate.** It sounds simple, and it is. But as you've likely experienced, simple doesn't mean easy. Most people don't get stuck because they don't know what to do. They get stuck because the moment they try to take action, their mind steps in.

They make a decision to move forward, and before they can even take the first step, their brain floods them with doubt, second-guessing, perfectionism, and every reason why it might not work.

Some people cycle endlessly between *Decide* and *Learn*, over-researching, over-analyzing, tweaking a strategy seventeen times, convincing themselves they're being thorough. But really, they're avoiding the most important step of all:

Implementation.

So, let's break this down and get honest about what it takes.

Decide
First, you decide. You choose one clear action to take next. Not the whole plan. Not the five-year roadmap. Just the next Pursuit Step.

And when you decide, decide fully. No half-decisions. No *"Well, maybe I'll try…"* Half-decisions create friction. They split your energy. They keep one foot in and one foot out.

Full decisions free up mental bandwidth. They unlock momentum. They tell your brain, *"This is what we're doing now. Period."*

And if your brain starts hissing, *"But what if it's the wrong decision?"* here's what I want you to remember. With the D.I.L.I. Method, there's no such thing as a wrong move. There is only action, and the data that action gives you.

Even a "flop" teaches you something that moves you closer to the result you want. Progress is not built on flawless execution. It's built on feedback.

Implement

Once you decide, implement quickly. This is where boldness meets behavior. This is where courage stops being a concept and starts becoming a muscle you actually flex. And sometimes (a lot of times), it won't feel good. At all.

One of my colleagues calls it *"gag and go,"* and I love that phrase because it's so real. This is the moment when your stomach is in knots, your brain is screaming, *"This is risky,"* and your inner critic grabs a megaphone to yell, *"Who do you think you are?"*… and you take the step anyway.

That's what builds capacity and courage. Action taken in the face of imperfection is how you train your nervous system to tolerate risk and navigate uncertainty. It's how you develop the emotional stamina required for bold pursuit.

Speed of implementation matters. The longer you sit in indecision, the louder your brain gets. It will hand you every excuse in the book for why you shouldn't move forward.

Don't give it that chance. Take the step. Even if it's small. Even if it's messy. Even if fear is hitching a ride in the passenger seat. Bold action rarely feels inspiring in the moment. It often feels awkward, uncomfortable, clumsy, terrifying. Do it anyway.

You don't have to feel fearless or "ready." You're building the capacity to act *in spite* of fear.

You're not building a life that looks perfect from the outside. You're building internal strength. You're building the mental, emotional, and spiritual strength that allows you to keep going, even when the outcome isn't guaranteed.

And when you fall (because you will), that's not failure. That's the process.

Think about how a baby learns to walk. They wobble. They fall. They faceplant. They cry. And then they try again. With every fall, they are literally building the balance, strength, and coordination needed to eventually walk with confidence.

The falling isn't a detour. It's the training.

Now imagine if we treated babies the way we treat ourselves: *"Oh wow, you fell again? Maybe walking's not for you."* It sounds ridiculous, right?

But this is exactly what so many of us do in pursuit. The first time something doesn't go perfectly, we spiral with thoughts like *"Maybe I'm not cut out for this."*

No. Maybe you're just in the part where you fall a lot. That part is sacred. It's building you.

The people who succeed aren't the ones who never fall. They're the ones who rise again and again. Every time they get back up, they build exactly the strength they need to walk their path with power.

Learn
Once you've implemented, it's time to learn. This part is non-negotiable. Learning is what transforms action into momentum. It's the difference between random effort and strategic growth.

Without this step, you're just throwing spaghetti at the wall and hoping something sticks. But when you pause to evaluate, you create a feedback loop that sharpens your skills, deepens your self-awareness, and brings you closer to your goal faster.

This is what keeps you in motion instead of stuck in frustration or self-doubt. Massive action isn't just about doing more. It's about doing, evaluating, and refining, until the result is inevitable.

Don't rush past this step. Take a moment to reflect:

- What worked?
- What didn't?
- What resistance came up?
- What surprised me?
- What could I do differently next time?

This is where growth lives. It's in the honest pause. It's in the willingness to examine your actions without judgment. That part is key because this is where most people self-sabotage. They hit an imperfect result and instantly attach meaning to it like, *"I failed. I'm not cut out for this. I knew I wasn't ready. I shouldn't have tried."* But that interpretation is optional.

An imperfect result doesn't mean anything about your value or your potential. It simply means you haven't figured it out… yet. You've found one more way that didn't work. That's actually valuable information because it helps you eliminate what doesn't work, refine your approach, and get closer to what does. You're in the process. You're gathering data. You're honing your strategy. Every single time you evaluate, you move one step closer to your goal with more clarity, precision, and power.

The only way to fail is to quit. Everything else is feedback.

Iterate
You learn. Then you iterate.

You take the insight, make a shift, and try again. This is how real progress is made. It doesn't happen in giant, cinematic leaps. It happens in small, consistent pivots. We move forward through the sacred loop of deciding, doing, learning, and adjusting.

This is why I teach that *massive action* doesn't mean going big once and praying it sticks. It means showing up with grit and curiosity, again and again, until the result is yours.

It's not about getting it right on the first try. You probably won't. Most people don't. That's okay, because the goal isn't perfection. The goal is becoming the version of you who keeps going without spiraling into self-judgment when things don't go as planned.

Let me show you what this looks like in real life.

Let's say you've been crushing it at work, but your physical health has taken a backseat. You're ready to change that. So, you commit to moving your body more.

Decide: You decide to add movement into your weekly routine starting now. You choose to go to the gym twice this week.

Implement: You block the time. Set out your clothes the night before. You show up, even if you're tired, even if it feels awkward, even if you're scared someone will judge how you look on the treadmill. (Gag and go, remember?)

Learn: At the end of the week, you reflect: *What worked? What made it harder? What helped me follow through? Did I enjoy the type of workout I chose? Was the time of day realistic? Where did my excuses pop up?*

We evaluate:

- **What worked:** setting out clothes the night before
- **What didn't work:** You only went to the gym once. Trying to go to two hour-long classes at the gym for both workout sessions wasn't realistic with your current schedule.
- **What will you do differently next week:** Do one class at the gym and one walk around the neighborhood to increase the likelihood of following through with 2 workouts

Iterate: You adjust. For week two, you'll still aim for two workouts, but one will be a gym class, and the other will be a 30-minute walk in your neighborhood. You text a friend to be your accountability buddy.

That's the D.I.L.I. Method in action, and that's how sustainable change happens. The goal isn't to go from zero to a perfect fitness routine in a week. The goal is to stay in the D.I.L.I. cycle, Decide, Implement, Learn, Iterate, until you create the desired outcome. That's how success is achieved and how real, lasting change is built.

And while you're iterating, here's something to keep in mind. Not all action is created equal.

One of the biggest traps people fall into is mistaking motion for progress. They spin in a frenzy of busyness, piling on action, thinking if they just *do enough*, something will eventually stick.

But spinning in 47 directions doesn't move you forward. It moves you into exhaustion and makes it difficult to evaluate the efficacy of your actions.

Constraint is a superpower. Focused pursuit beats scattered effort every single time. You don't need to master everything or chase every shiny opportunity. You need to get honest about what matters most *right now* and commit to moving toward it, one intentional step at a time.

When you stay in the D.I.L.I. loop, progress becomes inevitable. You gain valuable data and insight with every action. You learn what works, what doesn't, and what needs to shift. Each adjustment gets you closer to the result.

When you show up boldly, take messy action, and keep going, even when it's uncomfortable or unclear, you make success inevitable.

Big things get built through consistent, focused effort. This is how you move forward. This is how you make the impossible your new normal.

Compass Check:
- What goals am I truly committed to right now (pick 1 to 3)?
- What actions will create the most leverage toward those goals?
- What am I willing to say no to or set aside to keep myself focused and resourced?

Remember, constraint isn't about shrinking your dreams. It's about creating the space and clarity to pursue them with power. You can dream big, but you won't bring those dreams to life by scattering your focus and running yourself into the ground. As Greg McKeown writes in *Essentialism*, success isn't about doing more. It's about doing less, but better.

If you want to make meaningful progress, choose your targets wisely, stay focused, iterate like a scientist, and direct your energy toward what truly moves the needle. The people you admire didn't succeed by doing everything at once. They chose. They simplified. They focused their actions and moved with clarity and courage toward what mattered most.

That's exactly what you're learning to do here.

Lead the Pursuit Cycle: Build Capacity, Fuel Belief, Create Real Results

If there is one habit that makes bold pursuit sustainable and your goals inevitable, it is staying in what I call the *Pursuit Cycle.*

This is the engine behind real progress. The Pursuit Cycle keeps you moving toward what matters while developing the belief, capacity, and resilience required to achieve it. It is where bold action meets intentional belief and learning-driven iteration. When you know how to lead yourself through it consistently, you become unstoppable.

The trouble is, most people fall out of the Pursuit Cycle without even realizing it. It often looks like this. You take action. It feels hard. The result isn't what you hoped for. Your mind spins. You interpret the outcome as a reflection of your worth or potential. You begin to hesitate. You pull back. Your belief takes a hit. The quality of your actions declines. Your learning stalls. Before long, you are stuck in indecision, spinning in busyness, or avoiding the next step entirely.

What many people do not realize is that it is not the effort itself that burns them out, it's the mental judgment and self-doubt that follow. This is what it looks like when you slip out of the Pursuit Cycle.

Let me be clear. You cannot create extraordinary results from outside this cycle. When you operate from fear, doubt, or discouragement, you waste time and energy. You end up stuck in patterns of proving, perfecting, or performing. These patterns will leave you exhausted but no closer to what you truly want.

So, what does it look like to stay inside the Pursuit Cycle?

- Taking bold, learning-driven action using The D.I.L.I. Method.
- Intentionally managing belief as you go, choosing thoughts that fuel capacity, courage, and commitment.
- Extracting the highest level of learning from every iteration.
- Building resilience with every step, strengthening your ability to hold both uncertainty *and* belief in the inevitability of success.
- Maintaining momentum, even when the path feels hard.

The key is refusing to make any single outcome mean something about your worth or whether success is possible. That belief work is what keeps you inside the cycle and moving forward.

Let's compare that to what it looks like when you fall out of the Pursuit Cycle:

- Reacting to results instead of leading yourself through them.
- Spiraling in self-judgment.
- Action quality drops, you start playing small, hedging, hesitating.
- Learning stalls out and you stop extracting insights that would help you iterate better.
- Asking *"am I really capable of achieving this goal or creating this result?"* instead of *"what am I learning?"*
- Thinking about quitting instead of thinking about your best next step.

When you stay in the Pursuit Cycle, you keep moving forward with courage and clarity. You stay focused on learning, not proving. You manage your belief with intention, even when the external results aren't perfect... yet. You take progressively higher-quality actions that are better informed, more courageous, and more aligned with your ultimate goal. You build capacity, resilience, and the identity of someone who creates big things.

Make no mistake, this is a skill. This isn't just something you either have or don't. People aren't just born knowing how to lead themselves through the Pursuit Cycle (sure, maybe a few unicorns are, but don't use that as a reason to beat yourself up).

In Pursuit Insight:
Winners aren't the ones who never waver. They're the ones who keep putting themselves back in the game.

You build this skill just like any other—by practicing, repeating, getting coached as needed, and staying committed.

In my coaching work, I see this pattern every day. The ones who thrive aren't immune to doubt or fear. They've simply built the skill of noticing when their belief is slipping and know how to coach themselves back into alignment.

They recognize the early warning signs when their actions become more cautious. They spot the early signs that they are no longer learning from

136

their efforts and have started retreating into self-doubt or self-protection. Instead of spiraling, they recalibrate.

They understand that belief fuels the quality of their action. High-quality, belief-driven action leads to meaningful learning. The depth of that learning expands their capacity and strengthens their performance.

That is the Pursuit Cycle in motion. It is not about doing more. It is about doing *better*: better belief, better action, better learning. That is how you accelerate results.

When you notice your belief slipping, here's a quick and powerful way to clean it up.

Ask yourself four simple questions:

- What story am I telling myself right now?
- Is that story actually true?
- Is that story serving me or my pursuit?
- What would the story need to be in order to serve me better?

The goal here isn't to force yourself into positivity. It's to shift your mental frame toward a belief that is both true and useful, one that will fuel your next bold action rather than stall you out. Purposefully Derived Thoughts (the same ones we introduced in Chapter 5) can help to strengthen and anchor belief. These include questions like:

- What *do* I know?
- What *do* I understand?
- What *is* clear?
- What experience do I already have?
- Why will this be more effective?
- How will this add value?

These aren't affirmations. They're anchors. They pull your mind out of the fog and into a place of grounded clarity. They reconnect you with your power. Sometimes, that's all you need to take the next step. Sometimes it provides just enough clarity to move forward.

You can also use belief anchors. These are simple phrases or reminders that reconnect you to possibility and identity. They are the kind that remind you of who you are when fear is screaming. Here are some examples, but feel free to go wild and find the one(s) that work for you.

- *With enough time, energy, and attention, there's nothing I can't figure out.*
- *If the desire lives in me, the capacity to create it lives in me too.*
- *The process is the point. This is who I'm becoming.*
- *If I keep taking the next right action, success is inevitable. There is no rush.*

Then take the next bold Pursuit Step, one that is aligned with the belief you are building.

Let's return to the busy executive I mentioned earlier who was rebuilding her physical fitness.

In the beginning, she was moving beautifully through the Pursuit Cycle. She was setting clear targets, taking bold action, learning what worked for her body and schedule, and iterating with each new week.

But after a couple of weeks, when life got hectic and she missed a few workouts, her belief tanked.

She started telling herself, *"See? I can't stick with it. I'm not disciplined enough."* Her actions flatlined. She stopped scheduling gym time. She stopped reflecting on what had worked earlier. Her learning stalled out. She had quietly slipped out of the Pursuit Cycle and into the exact thought patterns that keep people stuck.

This is where the coaching came in. We cleaned up her belief first, not with blind positivity, but with thoughts that were true and useful, like: *"Missing a few workouts doesn't mean I can't do this. It means I need to adjust and recommit. I know how to get back on track."*

Then we identified the next bold Pursuit Step she could take.

In her case, it was simply scheduling her next workout and deciding to go, no matter how imperfect it felt. Once she did that, we extracted every bit of learning from the experience.

We asked high-quality questions like: *"What made it easier to follow through this time? What shifted when her belief was back in place?"*

From there, she iterated again, with stronger belief, clearer actions, and more resilience than before.

That's what it looks like to lead yourself back into the Pursuit Cycle on purpose. You clean up belief first. Then you take the next bold step.

You learn everything you can from what happens. Then you iterate and go again.

That's how you stay in motion. That's how you compound progress. That's how you build the capacity to create results you used to think were impossible. When you fall out of the Pursuit Cycle, so much time, energy, effort (and sometimes money) is wasted. You're tempted to think you need a new strategy, new planner, or a new system. But what you really need is to re-enter the Pursuit Cycle and lead yourself through it on purpose.

When you learn this skill, pursuit becomes sustainable, fun, aligned, fulfilling, and satisfying. It's also what makes success inevitable. You stop asking *"can I really do this?"* every five minutes. You start focusing on what you're learning and who you're becoming. You stop needing every action to be validated with an immediate perfect result. You start celebrating the process of becoming someone who knows how to create results. You stop spiraling when something doesn't work. You start iterating with courage and clarity. That's the Pursuit Cycle. And when you commit to leading yourself through it, you become the kind of person who can pursue big dreams with both boldness *and* joy, fully alive, fully capable, fully in pursuit.

Another common culprit that knocks people out of the Pursuit Cycle is when they hit resistance and *"just don't feel like it."* Basically, this is your brain throwing an *"I don't wanna"* toddler fit. It can be helpful to understand what's happening here. It's not that YOU don't want to, it's that your primitive brain is running the show.

The primitive brain is motivated to seek pleasure, avoid pain, and conserve energy. In modern-day pursuit, that wiring can sabotage you. It will seduce you with comfort and convenience and convince you that scrolling, snacking, or binging Netflix is safer than taking the risk of showing up. That's why you have to learn to supervise your own mind. You have to develop a new motivational system to seek growth, embrace discomfort, and expend massive effort wisely.

When you notice yourself saying *"I don't feel like it,"* pause and ask:

- Is this a genuine signal to rest or realign?
- Or is this my primitive brain trying to pull me toward false pleasure and comfort rather than growth and expansion?

Take a moment to remember what you want *most* vs what you want *now*. Breakthroughs and extraordinary results often live on the other side of resistance and boredom. When you expect that and lead yourself through it anyway, you stay inside the Pursuit Cycle. Even when it's hard.

Chapter 9:

SUSTAIN the Freedom

Being With the Not Yet: How to Live Now Without the Thing You're Chasing

A few years ago, my husband asked me, *"What's your biggest fear?"* Just your typical Saturday morning conversation over here at the Smarro household, no big deal.

I don't even remember what sparked it. I think we were standing by the kitchen island, him stirring coffee, me rummaging through the pantry for the oats I always swear we're out of. It felt like any other morning. Until it wasn't.

Ten years earlier, I would have rattled off a polished and well-rehearsed answer. It would have sounded impressive on a business podcast and made me seem like a high achiever. I might have said I feared failure, losing momentum, or wasting my potential. But that morning, a different truth slipped out, quietly, unpolished, and entirely unscripted.

"I'm afraid I'll never actually enjoy my life."

The words surprised even me. It wasn't that they weren't true, I'd just never heard them come out of my mouth. Until that moment, they'd lived buried beneath the noise of productivity and goal-setting. But now they were sitting right there between us, floating in the air like morning steam from his coffee. And as soon as I said it, I knew. That was the real fear.

On paper, I was living a life that a past version of me had dreamed of. It was a life I had once prayed for, written down in journals, visualized, and worked hard to create. But here I was, sitting inside that very life, and I was missing it. I was missing the joy, the fulfillment, the experience of living it.

To be fair, I wasn't completely missing it. There were times I could acknowledge and experience the beautiful moments, for sure: laughter around the dinner table, a quiet walk at sunset, moments of giddy delight where I felt like I was getting away with something simply by having a job that brought me so much joy, a post-coffee journaling session that made me feel more alive than anything else ever had.

I had joy, but not the deep, unshakable kind that seeps into your bones. The kind that roots itself beneath the surface and whispers, *"This is enough."* That kind of joy, soul-deep fulfillment, was something I couldn't access. Not fully. Not consistently. Not yet.

That conversation woke me up, and it led me to a truth that I now coach on constantly. If you don't learn how to live well with the "not yet," you will never feel satisfied, even when you achieve the thing you're chasing.

Here's an experience that is all too familiar to most high achievers. The minute they hit one milestone, they move the target. They're Olympic-level goalpost movers. They accomplish something meaningful on Monday, and by Wednesday, they're already chasing the next thing, minimizing the win, telling themselves it wasn't that big of a deal.

They're wired to focus on the gap between where they are and where they want to be. But if that's the only game you know how to play, the pursuit starts to feel empty. You become someone who is always chasing, never arriving. You become someone who is constantly pushing for more, but unable to fully experience what you already have.

That's not freedom. That's not fulfillment. That's not a satisfying life. Sustaining freedom means learning to live well now, even when the next thing you want hasn't happened yet.

It means learning to hold the paradox of having deep gratitude for what *is*, while also experiencing a deep desire for what *could be*. It means learning to live in the gap between where you are and where you want to be without making it mean something's gone wrong. It's choosing to stay present even when your brain is pitching a fit because you haven't hit the goal yet.

Presence over perfection isn't a motivational poster, it's a practice of radically deconditioning your brain from the lie that your worth lives in the outcome. You stop outsourcing your value to future results and start reclaiming it now, while everything's still unfolding.

The Trap of Conditional Living

One of the reasons people struggle with this is that they believe if they allow themselves to feel ease, contentment, or satisfaction *now*, they'll lose their edge. They'll stop striving. They won't be motivated to pursue the next goal.

I hear this all the time, especially when it comes to weight loss or body goals. Clients will resist loving or appreciating their bodies now because they think they need to fuel change with self-loathing or dissatisfaction. They think if they stop hating their body, they'll stop trying to change it.

But here's the truth. Self-loathing here will be self-loathing there. If you don't practice feeling alive, grateful, or confident now, you won't magically feel those things when you lose the weight or hit the revenue goal. You'll just move the line again.

Emotional maturity is realizing this. It's taking full ownership of your emotional experience and refusing to outsource your peace to a future outcome. Instead of believing *"I'll feel free when I lose the weight,"* or *"I'll feel peaceful when the business hits seven figures,"* or *"I'll feel alive when I meet my soulmate,"* it's about saying, *"I am the one who creates my internal state."* And then building the skill set to actually do it.

In Pursuit Insight:
If you can't feel it here, you won't feel it there. Learn to live now the way you think success will let you live later.

Anchoring joy, peace, or worth to a future milestone creates a loop of *conditional living*. Emotions become tethered to variables that are often unpredictable, like timelines, outcomes, or the behavior of others. It turns the present into a waiting room for the *"not yet."* The truth is, the feelings being chased later *could be cultivated now* through intentional focus, belief, and nervous system practices.

The magic of doing that work is this: when you no longer need the next win to feel alive, satisfied, or fulfilled, it gets a lot easier to see what you truly want. Your desires get cleaner and clearer. If you know you can create those emotional experiences for yourself, then you are free to pursue your goals from *pure desire* rather than lack.

And yes, sometimes that means certain goals no longer matter to you. And that's okay. In fact, that's clarity. If a goal only mattered because you believed it would buy you an emotional state you can now create for yourself, that goal was always a false promise. It was never going to give you what you truly wanted.

The work, then, is to create the emotional experience you want now, to feel ease, contentment, and gratitude right alongside ambition. To say, *"I can love my life today and still want to grow, evolve, and build tomorrow."* You're not choosing between satisfaction and success. You're learning to let one fuel the other.

This is the practice that makes pursuit sustainable. This is what allows you to stay in motion without collapsing into burnout or endless dissatisfaction. You are no longer using suffering to fuel achievement. You are using joy, curiosity, creativity, and freedom to fuel aligned pursuit. And that is how you begin to live in alignment long-term. Instead of chasing breakthrough after breakthrough you get to embody the freedom, fulfillment, and success you're here to create.

Nervous System Recalibration
But this isn't just a mindset shift. It's a nervous system shift.

This work also requires managing your nervous system and identity baseline. Here's what I mean by that. When you've been in high-achievement mode for a long time, your nervous system gets trained to expect that the "good life" is always one achievement away. You subconsciously tie your sense of fulfillment to the next external win.

If you're not careful, even extraordinary growth becomes invisible. Your nervous system adapts, and your brain normalizes your new level of success. Suddenly, what used to feel incredible now just feels like baseline. You stop feeling the gain because your focus is locked on the next gap.

That's why I coach clients to implement celebration rituals and why I often begin sessions with questions like, *"What's working? What do you want to celebrate today?" "What evidence do you have that you're getting closer to what you want?"* They help intentionally track progress. Otherwise, growth becomes the new stasis, and you lose connection to the joy of the life you've created.

Here are a few questions I love to give clients to zoom out, anchor into gratitude, and actually see the progress they're making:

- What can I celebrate right now that a past version of me would be thrilled about?
- What worked well this month that I want to do more of?
- Where can I recognize and honor the ways I've expanded?
- What was the best use of my time, energy, or talents, and how can I do more of that?

Without this practice, the pursuit itself can become a treadmill. You're running hard but feeling empty. With it, you build the skill of wanting what you have while still wanting more. And *that* is a skill. For some of us, it's the hardest one to learn.

Most of us are great at wanting more. We're good at ambition, vision, and future focus. What we're not great at is sitting inside our current life, fully present, fully grateful, fully alive, while allowing desire to coexist.

But this is how you create sustainable freedom and joy. You stop making "the next result" your only source of fulfillment. You anchor yourself in the experience of living well *now*, while pursuing more of what you love. The reflection questions above will help you do just that.

This is also a practice of nervous system recalibration. You teach your body and your mind that it is safe to feel good and experience satisfaction. It is safe to slow down enough to feel gratitude. It is safe to celebrate the gains.

When you do that, you actually become more powerful in pursuit, because you are no longer chasing from lack. You are creating from wholeness. You are pursuing from a foundation of *enough-ness*, not from a pit of *not-enough-yet*.

If I'm totally honest, the *"slow down and breathe"* advice used to make me want to roll my eyes. I mean, I tried the deep breaths. I journaled. I listened to the wellness podcasts and lit the dang candles. But somehow, I still felt like I was white-knuckling my life. Joy felt... distant. Like something I'd *maybe* feel after I crossed one more thing off the list.

Then I learned the truth.

If your nervous system is stuck in survival mode, it literally can't access joy... or connection, or even gratitude. Polyvagal Theory calls this the body's protective response.[4] It's not a character flaw. It's biology. Your system thinks it's under threat, so it's bracing itself with a tight jaw, shallow breath, constant alertness.

You're not failing at joy. Your body just doesn't feel safe enough for it.

That was a game-changer for me. Suddenly, those so-called "soft" practices, like pausing to feel the sun on my skin or taking three deep breaths before I rushed into another meeting, weren't just wellness fluff. They were *on-ramps to freedom.* They were the small, quiet ways I told my body, *"We're okay now. You can let go."*

Deb Dana calls those moments *"glimmers."*[5] They're not fireworks or full-on bliss. They're just little sparks of okay-ness. A lyric that hits just right. The smell of coffee that makes you sigh. A friend's text that makes you laugh-snort. Tiny cues of safety. She says when we notice them, linger with them, and name them, we start rewiring our system to expect good things. We learn to trust that joy is allowed.

Rick Hanson takes it a step further. He says we've got to install the good stuff because our brains are *Velcro for the negative and Teflon for the positive.*[6]

It's not enough to have a good moment. We've got to feel it on purpose. He encourages us to hold it in our awareness for at least 20 seconds. Let it land. That's how we train our brains to believe we're safe, supported, and enough.

Then there's Kristin Neff reminding us that none of it sticks without self-compassion.[7] If you don't learn how to talk to yourself like someone worth rooting for, no amount of breathing or glimmers will hold. You'll keep chasing the next win, the next milestone, the next scrap of proof that you're worthy. But when you learn to let joy land, when you stay with the good, when you treat yourself like someone who deserves celebration *right now*, that's when things shift.

---

[4] Stephen W. Porges, The Polyvagal Theory: Neurophysiological Foundations of Emotions, Attachment, Communication, and Self-Regulation (New York: W. W. Norton & Company, 2011).

[5] Deb Dana, The Polyvagal Theory in Therapy: Engaging the Rhythm of Regulation (New York: W. W. Norton & Company, 2018).

[6] Rick Hanson, Hardwiring Happiness: The New Brain Science of Contentment, Calm, and Confidence (New York: Harmony Books, 2013).

[7] Kristin Neff, Self-Compassion: The Proven Power of Being Kind to Yourself (New York: William Morrow, 2015).

You stop living like peace is something you have to *earn*. You stop treating your nervous system like it's a problem to fix. You start feeling free, right here in your body, your life, and this very moment.

The irony is that *this* level of presence and acceptance is what actually builds the strength and capacity to go even bigger. You become someone who can hold success and still savor the present. You chase dreams from fullness, not from fear.

That's what I want for you. A life where joy doesn't wait its turn. A life where a hijacked nervous system isn't running the show. A life where the pursuit itself is infused with freedom. Where growth and gratitude walk hand in hand. Where success isn't just something you hit once, but something you learn how to feel every single day.

Compass Check:
- Where am I still telling myself I can't feel satisfied until something changes?
- What emotional experience do I want most, and how can I practice feeling that now?
- How would my pursuit change if I pursued from wholeness instead of from lack?

Joy, Rest, and Play as Strategy

A few years ago, I found myself sitting on a beach in Mexico, supposedly on vacation. The sun was dipping into the ocean, the kind of scene people dream about. I had my laptop in my bag *just in case,* and I kept checking my phone between sips of a margarita I didn't even really want. My shoulders were still tense. My mind was still buzzing with to-do lists and undone tasks.

And I remember thinking, *Why can't I feel this? Why can't I enjoy what I worked so hard to create?*

That moment revealed something I hadn't been willing to see before. I realized I had been carrying an unspoken rule for years. I believed rest, joy, and play had to be earned. They were rewards, not requirements. I treated them like little perks I could enjoy *after* proving myself.

Rest came after I finished the hard stuff. Joy was something I allowed myself when I hit a milestone. Play was reserved for rare occasions when everything else was done.

And because there was always something more to do, I rarely felt like I had permission to feel good. It took practice to undo that pattern.

I started small. I scheduled guilt-free walks in the middle of the day. I gave myself permission to laugh at a dumb Netflix show *before* the work was finished. I tracked how I felt, not just what I accomplished. And slowly, I noticed something shift.

The more I built joy, rest, and play into my daily life, the more energized, creative, and grounded I became. It was not fluff. It was fuel. What I know now is that these things are not optional. They are not extra. They are strategy.

Joy, rest, and play are what make the pursuit sustainable. They are what keep you connected to yourself in the middle of the hustle. They remind you that life is not just about the goal, it's about how you feel *while you're creating it*.

Burnout doesn't come from doing too much. It comes from doing all of it without joy, without pause, without remembering that you are a human being, not a machine.

If you want to create something extraordinary, you have to learn to protect the energy that makes it possible. You have to build a life that feels good *now*, not just when you cross the finish line.

Finding Your Unique Rhythm

What sustains your freedom may not look like what sustains mine. That's why I don't offer cookie-cutter formulas, rigid routines, or bulletproof schedules. I don't believe in copy-paste blueprints, because true freedom doesn't come from outsourcing your rhythm. It comes from building the skill of listening inward. It comes from learning to notice what makes you feel most alive, most resourced, most powerful in pursuit.

One of the tools that helped me tap into this kind of inner listening was Human Design.

Now, I'm not here to tell you to dive into the charts or memorize gates and channels. I'm not a Human Design expert. But I *am* a sacral generator, and learning what that meant, and how my energy responds to what lights me up, changed everything.

It helped me stop bulldozing through decisions that felt heavy just because they *"should"* make sense. It helped me stop draining my energy on strategies that didn't feel alive. When I started tuning into that internal yes, that spark that said, *"This is yours"*, I pursued with more ease, more flow, and more fire. And then something wild happened.

I ran a little experiment in my business. I decided to follow what lit me up. I gave myself permission to say no to the heavy, misaligned *"shoulds"* and say yes to what made me feel excited, creative, and deeply energized.

That month, I had my first five-figure month.

Coincidence? Maybe. But honestly, it's a lot more fun if I *don't* see it that way (see how that whole *"thoughts aren't facts"* thing can work *for* us?!). Sometimes the most empowering shift is just deciding your life gets to make sense in a way that *feels* good to you.

When you pursue from alignment, joy, and energy, you move faster and cleaner than when you pursue from duty and depletion.

In Pursuit Insight:
Your pursuit isn't meant to look like anyone else's. Own what fuels you. Run your race. That's how you win your life.

Here's a question I invite you to sit with: *What do the feelings of aliveness and freedom actually feel like for you?* What brings you that feeling? I'm not talking about what lights you up in *theory*, or what your favorite influencer says, or what your best friend does. I'm not even asking you to consider what past-you assumed.

I'm inviting you to ask, *what is it now?*

For me, I thought my version of aliveness would be floating in a pool with a cold drink and a good book. And listen, I *do* love that. If you know me, you know I literally travel with a floaty. No shame.

Friend's pool party? Floaty in the back seat. Mastermind event at a Vegas hotel? Travel floaty in the suitcase. I'm not even kidding.

What surprised me was realizing that my deepest sense of aliveness doesn't come from lounging. It comes from *meeting a challenge*. I feel most alive when I'm growing or working on something that stretches me.

I come alive when I am learning new skills, running new races, or pushing into edges that call something greater out of me.

I used to think that rest and joy would mean turning down the fire, easing the pace, or coasting. But the truth is, what lights me up is living fully on purpose in ways that call me to expand into untapped areas of myself.

That realization changed the way I define *balance*. It helped me stop trying to force myself into other people's versions of self-care. I stopped chasing someone else's cadence. I stopped mimicking the energy of people who weren't wired like me. And in that process, I reclaimed my own.

That is the invitation I'm extending to you. Get curious about your energy. Pay attention to your joy. Learn the nuances of what fuels you and what depletes you. Start by asking yourself questions like

- What kind of rest actually restores me?
- What kind of play cracks me open with laughter or creativity?
- What kind of challenge brings me to life?
- What kind of environment helps me thrive?

When you understand your own energetic fingerprint, you become a better steward of your freedom. You make better decisions. You stop defaulting to hustle as the only valid form of progress, and you build a life that supports you back.

The Foundation of Sustainable Pursuit
Too many of us wear overwork like a badge of honor. We confuse exhaustion with effectiveness, but constant striving without joy is unsustainable. Pushing forward without rest is risky. Grinding without play will strip the freedom right out of your life.

You are not a machine or a robot. You are a living, breathing, beautiful complexity of energy, emotion, creativity, and calling. You cannot sustainably run on output alone. So treat joy, rest, and play as non-negotiable components of your performance strategy. They're not extras or rewards. *They're foundational.*

This isn't about taking random bubble baths, unless, of course, that lights you up. (It absolutely does for me. I'm picking up on a water theme.) This is about something deeper. It's about understanding that your most potent pursuit doesn't come from grind mode. It comes from alignment.

Your nervous system, energy, and heart are the tools to lead with. When those are cared for, you become unstoppable. Joy is fuel. Rest is strategy. Play is capacity-building.

Freedom isn't just the ability to pursue what matters. It's the ability to enjoy the pursuit while you do it. And that requires conscious choices about how you spend your time, where you direct your energy, and what practices you build into your daily and weekly life. Each week, I recommend this simple practice. Schedule one experience that brings you joy. Schedule one experience of rest. (I'm talking about *real* rest here, the kind that restores you, not the kind that numbs you out.) And schedule one experience of play. Something just for the fun of it, with no productive outcome, no performance goal, and no hidden agenda.

If you're a little skeptical about the efficacy and efficiency this will lead to, that's okay. I was too. I invite you to approach this like a scientist running an experiment. You're collecting data and testing the hypothesis that following your unique design, and what lights you up, will lead to more success.

I'm talking about the kind of success that feels invigorating while chasing it, fulfilling while achieving it, and nourishing while sustaining it. This is not indulgence. This is *maintenance*. This is *what energetic leadership* looks like.

You don't have to be in pursuit like anyone else. You don't have to run yourself into the ground to prove you're worthy. You don't have to keep up with someone else's highlight reel. Your freedom is yours to define. Your energy is yours to protect. Your life is yours to lead.

When you stop trying to copy someone else's way and start honoring your own, you create a pursuit that is sustainable, repeatable, and deeply satisfying. This is leadership of self. This is maturity in pursuit. This is honoring the wisdom of your body and your spirit.

And here's an added bonus. You don't just do this for you. You do it for everyone watching, your clients, your team, your kids, your community. They're learning how to pursue by watching how *you* pursue. If they see someone building success at the expense of their peace, they will believe that's the cost. But if they see someone building success through joy, rest, and play, they will begin to believe that freedom is possible *on the path.*

When you live and lead in this way, you give those who are watching permission to do the same.

And that, my friend, is leadership.

Compass Check:
- What actually makes me feel alive in pursuit?
- What kind of rest genuinely restores me?
- Where am I still hustling out of habit instead of tuning into what lights me up?
- This week, how will I intentionally practice joy, rest, and play as strategy?

Freedom Is a Practice: The Skill of Continuous Recalibration

If there's one truth I want you to carry with you as we close this chapter, it's this: freedom is not a destination you arrive at and unpack your bags. It's not a certificate you earn after enough healing, hustling, or hoop-jumping.

Freedom is a practice. It's a living, breathing rhythm you commit to, again and again, as you evolve.

You don't arrive and stay there by default. You create it on purpose. And then you recreate it. You recalibrate as life shifts, as your desires expand, as new responsibilities stretch you into new edges. You lead yourself into freedom, not once, but over and over.

That's the hidden paradox in all this. Freedom isn't a static state. The more you grow, the more your version of freedom must grow with you. What once felt liberating might start to feel confining. What once sparked aliveness might now ask to be released. That's not a sign that there's a problem. It means you're still becoming.

I see this all the time in my work. Clients do the deep mindset work. They dismantle survival patterns, heal old stories, and choose a new identity. They step into the kind of life that once felt impossible. They start to experience more peace, more presence, and more possibility.

And then a new season comes. They venture into new levels in their business. They start a new relationship. They step onto larger stages with bigger audiences. A deeper calling lands on their heart. Suddenly the tools, thoughts, and habits that once supported them start to feel like ill-fitting clothes, and they panic.

They ask me, *"Why is this hard again? I thought I was past this."* But those are the wrong questions.

The real question is, *"What season am I in now, and who do I need to become to lead myself through it?"*

That discomfort and friction doesn't mean you've gone backward or failed. It means you've outgrown your current container. It means you're expanding, and expansion demands recalibration.

It's the same reason a six-figure entrepreneur can't scale to seven or eight figures by doing what they've always done. The skills, systems, roles, rhythms, and mindset that built one level can't carry the next. The business has to evolve. The leadership must stretch. How you manage your time, energy, and priorities has to evolve.

The same is true in your personal growth and freedom. The patterns of thought and action that served you beautifully at one stage may feel clunky or constricting at the next.

What got you here might not get you there, and that's not a problem. That's the process. Recalibration is not a setback. It's a signal of growth.

In Pursuit Insight:
If it feels harder, good. It means you're growing. Don't quit. Recalibrate.

This is why I teach continuous recalibration as a core skill. It's not glamorous. It's not flashy. But it's how you stay free while you grow. It's how you hold your expansion without collapsing under it.

And one of the tools I return to over and over, for myself and my clients, is the S.T.E.A.R. model: Situation → Thought → Emotion → Action → Result. This isn't a worksheet you fill out once and forget. It's a living compass. It's a recalibration ritual you can use anytime you feel stuck, stretched, or off course.

Every time you step into something new, a bigger stage, a bolder ask, a more intimate relationship, you get to ask:

- Am I still thinking thoughts that serve the future I'm building?
- Are the emotions I'm sitting in creating the energy I need?
- Are my actions aligned with who I say I want to become?
- Am I dragging old patterns into new seasons and wondering why it doesn't feel like freedom anymore?

The identity that served you at one level may need to stretch or soften or mature in the next. The beliefs that once protected you may now restrict you. The habits that once created safety may now block intimacy, risk-taking, or visibility. That's not because there's something wrong with you or because the next pursuit isn't for you. It's because you're growing, and growth demands regular, intentional recalibration.

So, every quarter, every month, or whenever life starts to feel tight, you can sit down and ask:

- What am I pursuing now?
- What's the life I'm building?
- What thoughts, emotions, and actions align with that?
- What needs to be released to make space for what's next?

This is how you stay in relationship with your freedom. You approach it as a living practice rather than a finish line. This is how you build the muscle of self-leadership. You stop expecting the old map to carry you into new territory, and you become the cartographer of your own evolution.

Expansion Tracking
Another essential piece of sustaining freedom is making your progress visible. You can't integrate what you don't witness, and what you don't integrate, you'll stay disconnected from.

The truth is, we normalize success at lightning speed. We move the goalpost before we've even caught our breath. We dismiss wins that would have once blown our own mind. That's why I teach a practice called *Expansion Tracking*. It's simple, but it's powerful.

At its core, Expansion Tracking is about intentionally noticing, honoring, and celebrating the ways you're growing, both internally and externally. It's a way to ground yourself in the truth of your evolution so your system can actually feel the growth, not just achieve it.

Every week, or month, or moon cycle (you do you), you ask yourself:

- What progress am I proud of?
- Where am I showing up in ways I used to only dream about?
- What internal shifts have I made (in how I think, feel, or act)?
- What results am I living that once felt impossible?

When you do this regularly, you rewire your nervous system to hold success. You allow joy to land. You build the capacity to feel fulfilled instead of constantly chasing the next thing in a void of not-enoughness.

In this process, you become more resilient. Because when the hard seasons come (and they will), you have a well of self-trust to draw from. You've trained yourself to see your own strength. You've witnessed your own becoming.

This is the true heartbeat of freedom. It's not in the mountaintop moments, but in the daily decision to walk yourself home to who you are becoming, again and again. You don't get there by force. You get there by presence.

That looks like showing up in the laundry-folding, hard-conversation-having, risk-taking, joy-feeling moments of your real life.

You get there by catching the expansion in real time. This looks like noticing when you say the thing you used to swallow. Acknowledging when you pitch the project you used to shrink from. Experiencing when you let joy in on a Thursday afternoon while mopping the floor with your favorite song playing.

You start letting those moments register, letting them shape your self-concept into someone who is living the life they once hoped for, one choice at a time. That's where freedom happens.

This process is about trusting that you will keep recalibrating, keep rising, not because you have to prove anything, but because *that's who you are*. That's what will sustain your freedom for the long game.

It's no longer about an arbitrary future achievement. It's about the way you walk yourself through this moment and the next.

As we close this part of the book, this is what I want you to carry forward. You are not starting from scratch. You are building from wisdom, from wins, from muscle memory. You have tools. You have truth. You know how to lead yourself now, not from pressure, but from presence. You are no longer chasing freedom from a place of lack. You are pursuing from alignment, sufficiency, and strength.

That is the practice. That is the path. And you're already on it.

Compass Check:
- Where in my life or pursuit am I feeling the need for a recalibration?
- What old thoughts or patterns might I need to release to move forward with more freedom?
- How am I tracking and celebrating my growth, and am I letting it land?
- What will sustaining freedom look and feel like in this next season of my life?

PART III:

THE PURSUIT

Becoming While Becoming

Chapter 10:

In Pursuit, Not Imprisoned

Pursuit as Sacred Exploration: The Real Point of the Pursuit

I once believed that alignment meant finding the *right* job. To me, that meant the perfect title and the dream position that would finally feel like a good match.

When I moved from Iowa to Texas, I didn't want to arrive without something lined up, so I accepted a "good on paper" position as the director of a psychiatric partial hospitalization program. It checked all the boxes. It sounded impressive. It paid decently well. But within 30 days, I had typed up a letter of resignation. I didn't send it, yet. I stayed a few more months out of loyalty and logistics, but in my gut, I already knew this wasn't it.

The next two roles were supposed to be *it*. Years earlier, I sat at a White House roundtable on jail diversion where these two organizations were held up as national models. Back then, I remember thinking, *If I could just be part of something like that, doing meaningful work at one of the country's gold-standard programs, I'd feel fulfilled in my career.*

Fast forward a few years, and there I was, in leadership positions at both of them. I had arrived… right?

Wrong.

What I found wasn't alignment, it was disillusionment. These programs were everything past-me would have drooled over. But from the inside, they felt off. The work itself was meaningful, but it no longer felt like *my* work. I could sense a quiet shift happening in me, an inner nudge that was growing harder to ignore.

It wasn't the kind of knowing that screams. It was the kind that whispers. The kind that shows up like a tug in your chest or a knowing in your gut. *Go back to direct care. Be with people again. It's time.*

It didn't make logical sense. I had worked so hard to move "up" in leadership and program development. I'd built a career on strategy, systems, and scale. But now, something deeper in me was calling, not toward another credential or job title, but toward a truer version of me.

Then came the wild hair.

During lockdown, with too much time and too many questions, I decided to get certified as a life coach. At the time, it was just a curiosity, something to explore for my own personal development. *Why not?* But once I got in… I fell in love. This wasn't just a new skill, it was a soul tap. I felt like I'd learned the secrets of the Universe. And once again, the nudge returned, stronger now:

Go all in.

Say what?! I'd never been an entrepreneur. I didn't even have the bug. Back in my jail diversion days, when other communities wanted to contract directly with me for program development and consultation, I routed everything through my employer. I liked safety, structure, and security.

But this time there was a deeper knowing. I had a sense that there were parts of me that had never been explored or expressed, and that stepping into full-time coaching might call those pieces forward. I had a sense that things I couldn't even name yet would become possible if I just followed the next *yes*.

Sure, I wanted to share the gospel of coaching. Of course, I wanted a business that was financially successful. But it was more than that. I wanted to become the version of me that existed on the other side of the leap.

So, I jumped again. I walked into my boss's office with a letter of resignation in hand. It was the fourth time in four years. But this time, it wasn't about running from the wrong thing. It was about walking toward the right one.

Each of those leaps wasn't just about changing jobs. They were clues. Each resignation was a breadcrumb, guiding me closer to something I couldn't yet name. I was no longer chasing roles or résumés. I was chasing *resonance*. I wasn't just pursuing a career. I was pursuing *myself*. That's why, when the idea for this book arrived, it felt familiar.

It didn't come as a lightning bolt. There was no perfectly formed outline. It was more like a quiet nudge that wouldn't go away, a steady internal pull that said, *"Hey, you know you want to do this. You just haven't owned it yet."* I recognized it. It was the same nudge that pulled me through those four jobs. The same nudge that told me the pursuit wasn't over; it was evolving.

I kept circling back to the same idea. We are designed to pursue. It's not just a function of ambition or a trait of high performers. It's part of our wiring. We are made in the image of a Creator, and at our core, we are creators too.

Whether or not we always feel like it, that creative pulse lives inside each of us. It hums beneath our obligations, our identities, and our fears. Sometimes it roars. Sometimes it flickers. But it's always there.

Just as God (Spirit, Source, the Divine, Highest Self, True Nature, use whatever language draws you closer) is always in pursuit of us, gently guiding us back to wholeness, we're also meant to live in pursuit too. Not in frantic striving, but in sacred, intentional movement. We're here to create what only *we* can bring into the world. That's not ego. That's how we're built.

The desire to grow, to contribute, to turn our lived experiences into something meaningful, that's the Divine impulse working through us.

The pursuit of success is not wrong or superficial. The pursuit of excellence, growth, expansion, and impact is not only valid, it's holy. You wouldn't be reading this if there wasn't a part of you that knew you were made for something bigger. That pull to grow, to create, to leave your mark, that's your purpose calling you. That's your God-given drive saying, *"Let's go."*

But here's where it gets messy.

Somewhere along the way, we were handed a broken blueprint. *Hustle harder. Stay busy. Never let 'em see you sweat.* We started measuring our worth by our output, sacrificing sleep, joy, even sanity, because somewhere we picked up the idea that burnout equals value.

So, we push. We strive. We perform. And we don't even notice that we've left ourselves behind. We don't mean to. But we do it. That's why this work matters. Because the goal isn't just to succeed, it's to succeed without abandoning yourself in the process.

Sacred pursuit, the kind that breathes life into your spirit and flow into your work, isn't about chasing an identity. It's about revealing the one you already have. It's not about becoming someone else. It's about becoming more fully *you*—more connected, more honest, more alive. Pursuit at its highest level is a spiritual practice of becoming. It's a process of remembering who you are and choosing to live and create from that place. Pursuit is sacred exploration of you.

This is why alignment matters so much. I first learned this on the mat during my Anusara yoga teacher training. Anusara is a heart-centered, alignment-based style of yoga. We weren't taught to force ourselves into poses or contort our bodies just to "achieve" a shape. The goal wasn't to master the perfect inversion or crush Warrior III. The real aim was to develop a relationship with alignment.

We were taught to discover our own "optimal blueprint." This refers to the unique, ideal alignment that supports strength, ease, and sustainable movement for your body. Then, the challenge was to maintain that alignment through every posture, every wobble, and every edge.

The pose itself was never the point. The postures were just opportunities, like math word problems, to apply the formula. The real work was building the strength to stay in alignment no matter how the shape changed.

I think back to those years of jumping jobs. Each one was a new shape I thought I had to master. But the real transformation came when I stopped trying to contort myself into the perfect role and started asking, *What's the truest version of me that wants to come through here?*

I started to realize this wasn't just about yoga. It was about life, business, and creativity too. *What if the goal isn't the point at all? What if success isn't a destination but a way of moving through the world? What if the real invitation is to stay anchored in your essence while stepping boldly into new pursuits?*

Maybe it's not just about what you're building, but about *who* you're becoming as you build it. Maybe the point is to stay present with what it feels like to be this version of you, the version who is bringing these ideas to life, creating these offerings, and expressing what's ready to come through.

Maybe alignment isn't just a practice on the mat, but a way of living that turns every pursuit into a deeper relationship with yourself and something greater.

The "pose" might be the business you're building, the book you're writing, or the family you're raising, but the deeper practice is staying in integrity with your alignment as you move. Your essence is not meant to be sidelined in the name of achievement. It's meant to be expressed *through* it.

Your offerings, creations, and goals are not random. They're an extension of the Divine expression moving through you. They are yours to bring into the world. But if you disconnect from yourself in the process, you've missed the point.

Pursuing success isn't about becoming worthy. You don't need to do that, because you already are. Worthiness is your starting place, not a finish line. It's inherent. You can't hustle your way into it, and you can't lose it by missing a milestone.

Being in pursuit of your version of success is about becoming more fully expressed. It's about letting what's within you take shape out in the world, and staying present to what it feels like to be *you* while doing it.

In my experience, the most powerful creations come when you're not just producing an outcome but actively participating in the act of *becoming*.

The deepest impact you'll ever make won't come from effort alone. It will come from *presence*. It will come from being fully *you* while doing the thing, not from losing yourself to do it better.

Sometimes the real point of pursuing a goal isn't the outcome, it's who you become in the process. Goals have a way of calling forward parts of you that have been quiet or untapped. They stretch how you think, how you create, and how you relate to yourself. They ask you to develop new skills, revisit old ones, and expand your sense of what's possible. They challenge you to build a self-concept that's not limited by your past, but lit up by who you're becoming.

That's why I remind my clients that the most important thing isn't whether they hit the goal with precision. The number, the title, and the revenue are just data points. What really matters is how you show up in the becoming.

Sometimes the deeper win isn't the result itself. It's the courage you cultivated, the clarity you accessed, and the capacity you built along the way. The growth, the fortitude, and the self-trust you build by showing up fully is what lasts. That's what changes you. And often, that internal transformation is the real success.

That's what excites me most about any goal: the version of me I'll grow into on the other side. I didn't know it then, but each resignation letter was a step in becoming. It wasn't just a career move. It was a deeper kind of commitment, to myself, to truth, and to the version of me I was still uncovering.

In Pursuit Insight:
You think you're chasing the finish line, but really, you're meeting a new version of yourself along the way. That's the real thrill of pursuit: the stretch, the becoming, the sacred friction of expansion.

When you pursue from a place of alignment and self-trust, everything changes. The energy shifts. The pursuit itself becomes a sacred practice. You're no longer chasing something outside of yourself. You're revealing what's already within. You're not striving to *"get there"* to feel worthy, whole, or complete. You're walking with the Divine, uncovering the truth, step by step. Each move deepens your relationship with who you already are.

My optimal blueprint isn't a strategy or a checklist. It's not a perfectly crafted five-year plan. It's a way of being that feels rooted and real. For me, it's deeply spiritual. When I talk about alignment, I'm pointing to that unshakable part of me that's grounded in love, truth, and grace. It's the part that's both created by and connected to something bigger–God, Spirit, Creator, Universe, Self-energy, Source, Wisdom, or simply Truth. Whatever name you use, the pulse is the same.

When I'm tapped into that place, I move differently. I create from trust instead of fear. I pursue from sufficiency rather than scarcity. I don't feel like I'm performing or proving. I feel like I'm co-creating with the Divine.

The practice is to pause, often. Before setting goals, before saying yes, before taking action, pause and ask: *Am I connected to my optimal blueprint right now? Is this choice coming from truth or ego? Is this next step aligned with who I actually am?* When I pause long enough to check in, everything downstream feels clearer, more grounded, and more me.

I have learned this lesson through experience in both business and life. I have achieved goals that appeared impressive to others but left me feeling disconnected from myself. I have pursued success in ways that looked good on the outside while feeling unsatisfied on the inside. I have said yes when I meant no, simply because the applause drowned out my intuition.

I witness this pattern often. Clients achieve incredible things but feel exhausted and unfulfilled. Friends receive admiration yet quietly admit to feeling numb. Leaders are praised for their productivity but confess they can no longer feel joy in their accomplishments.

At first glance, it seems like everything is working. The goals are being met. The milestones are being reached. The world is cheering. But internally, something feels off. There is a growing heaviness. Excitement fades. Tasks that once inspired energy now feel draining. People continue chasing goals that look good on paper but offer no real fulfillment.

Many of us have been taught that discipline means pushing through discomfort at all costs. However, true discipline sometimes means pausing long enough to ask better questions. It means having the courage to step back and acknowledge, *"This no longer feels aligned with who I am."*

The signals often show up long before full burnout arrives. The body begins to feel tired. Resentment simmers beneath the surface. Motivation fades. Joy disappears from activities that once brought excitement. These experiences are not signs of laziness or weakness. They are valuable data points that should not be ignored.

Ignoring those signals does not reflect strength. It reflects disconnection. The path forward is not to push harder. The path forward is to stop, breathe, and return to yourself. Ask yourself: *What is mine to give? What do I actually want to create right now? What would it feel like to pursue from sufficiency instead of scarcity?*

This is not giving up. This is a return to integrity.

When you reconnect to your why, your values, your vision, and your deeper Self, the energy shifts. Things start to feel a little more fun and magical. You remember what matters. You let go of what doesn't. Action becomes lighter, cleaner, more aligned.

You pursue because you want to, not because you feel like you have something to prove, and *that's* when the best stuff flows. That's when the pursuit feels expansive and free, rather than tight, anxious, and laced with self-doubt.

When it comes to high-quality living, the energy you pursue from will always matter more than the pose you strike for the world.

Pursuit, at its highest level, isn't about chasing validation or accumulating achievements. It's about expressing what's uniquely yours to give. It's about bringing your ideas, your voice, your gifts into the world in ways that are both meaningful and life-giving.

Your goals, dreams, and success aren't just about accomplishment. They're about contribution. They're about honoring what lives within you and choosing to shape it into something real, valuable, and true.

That's what sacred pursuit is. It's a devotion to growth, a commitment to expression, and a conscious decision to let your work reflect who you are and what you stand for.

Sometimes that something looks like a company or a podcast or a global movement. Sometimes it looks like rocking your baby to sleep or holding your friend's grief without flinching. Sometimes it looks like showing up to a blank page or a blank canvas and giving form to what you feel.

Sometimes it's wildly visible. Sometimes no one sees but you. But it's all sacred. Whether you're inventing tech that solves a worldwide problem, teaching third graders how to believe in themselves, or crafting a meal that brings your family together, what matters is that it's yours to give, and that you offer it from the center of who you are.

That's the sacred pursuit.

When you live from that place, when you choose expression over ego, presence over performance, integrity over impression, everything changes. You stop trying to earn your way into belonging. You realize *you already belong*, and that shifts the entire pursuit from pressure to power.

You were made for this. You were made to express and reveal. You are a creator by nature. When you honor the creative impulse within you, you're not just building something. You're becoming someone. Someone more true. Someone more whole. Someone more alive.

I believe every one of us arrives on this planet packed with raw potential. But having it doesn't guarantee you'll use it. *That part is on you.* You have to decide. You have to choose which pieces of that potential you're going to pursue. It's a conscious decision about who you want to become, what you're willing to lean into, and how boldly you'll chase the version of you that hasn't fully emerged yet.

For a long time, I thought I was doing that. I climbed the ladder. I landed the jobs. I said yes to the things that looked like progress. But after walking away from four roles in four years, including some that were supposed to be the pinnacle, I started to realize something deeper. Potential doesn't just live in titles or upward trajectories. It lives in alignment. It lives in what you dare to say yes to, even when it doesn't make sense on paper.

That same choice was true long before my professional life ever started. I didn't grow up with a playbook for personal development. I grew up around addiction and incarceration. For years, it felt like survival was the goal. But even then, something in me knew there was more.

That knowing, the desire to see what else was possible, became my earliest form of pursuit.

If you're looking for a compass to guide that pursuit, start with your desire. Your deepest, most honest desires are not random, they're the map.

Picture a Venn diagram. One circle is *desire*, the other is *potential*. Where they overlap, *that's your life*. That's where purpose lives. That's where your fullest expression and real impact start to take shape.

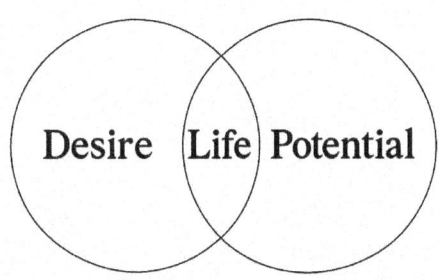

The magic isn't just in what you *can* do. It's in what you *want* to do and what you *choose* to do, even when it's hard. The real thrill of being alive is found in the exploration of what's possible. That's the pursuit. That's where you get to decide that every challenge, hardship, or disadvantage is actually *for* you. It's part of your curriculum. It's how you build the skills and the stamina to relentlessly chase your potential.

And that, my friend, that is sacred.

Compass Check:
- What is your optimal blueprint?
- How does alignment with Source, Self-Energy, or True Nature feel in your body, your thoughts, your choices?
- Are you making decisions from pressure, or from presence

Practice checking in regularly, not only when things feel off, but as a sacred rhythm for how you lead yourself through every pursuit.

Time as an Ally, Not a Trap

Let's talk about one of the most subtle but persistent ways people accidentally imprison themselves in the pursuit of success. It's their relationship with time.

I see it constantly. Brilliant, purpose-driven, passionate humans who've built lives that look admirable on paper, but underneath the surface, there's this low-grade hum of anxiety that never seems to turn off. It's not always loud, but it's ever-present, like a fluorescent light buzzing in the back of the mind:

There's not enough time. I'm already behind. There's too much to do. I wasted today. I'm wasting my life.

I get it. I've felt it too. The world doesn't exactly slow down to hand you a breather. Your ambitions are real. Your calendar is full. Your responsibilities are many. So, if you're not intentional, it's incredibly easy to slip into a warped relationship with time, one where time is no longer the space you get to live in; it becomes something you're losing. It becomes something you're chasing, something that slips through your fingers every time you try to grip it tighter.

And when that shift happens, when time becomes a thief or a threat, your pursuit starts to contort. It no longer feels like a bold, soul-led adventure. It becomes a frantic scramble. It starts to feel like a panicked race, a never-ending sprint that leaves you gasping for air even as you keep checking boxes and chasing goals.

If you've ever sat at your desk with twenty-six tabs open, toggling between tasks while your brain shouts 183 other things you haven't done yet, you know what I mean. Or maybe your version is more internal, an endless loop of mental *should* playing on repeat:

I should have started earlier. I should be further by now. I should be able to do this faster. I shouldn't have wasted that hour scrolling. I should already be done.

But what I've learned is this. When your pursuit starts to feel like a race against time, you're no longer moving from freedom. You're moving from fear. And no matter how much you accomplish from that place, it will never feel like enough, because it's not just the tasks that drain you, it's the story you're living inside while doing them.

I had to come face-to-face with this in my own journey. For years, I carried this quiet but constant belief that I was behind. *Behind what,* exactly? I couldn't say. But the feeling lived in my body like background noise.

It didn't matter how much I accomplished. The to-do list regenerated daily. The pace never felt sustainable. And then I'd look around at other entrepreneurs, creators, parents, leaders and think, *They're doing more. They're building faster. They've got five lifetimes squeezed into one. Meanwhile, I'm over here trying to keep up with just one.*

And when I told myself I was behind, my nervous system responded accordingly. I pushed harder. I slept less. Said yes too often. Hustled more.

And the result was not magical. It didn't lead to epic breakthroughs or exponential impact. The result was burnout, creative numbness, and a deeper entanglement with the very story I was trying to outrun.

What finally started to shift things for me wasn't a new time-blocking method or productivity
hack. It was a complete reframe of what it meant to *use* time well.

The 8 Cs and 5 Ps Framework
One of the most anchoring beliefs I hold now is this: time is always well spent when it's used to access the 8 Cs and 5 Ps.

Let me explain. In Internal Family Systems (IFS), a modality that's deeply shaped how I serve and live, there are qualities that emerge when you're operating from Self-energy, aka the most aligned, integrated version of you.

The 8 Cs of Self-Energy
These are the core qualities that arise when you're in true Self-leadership:

- **Calm** – Steady in the storm, unshaken by chaos

- **Clarity** – Seeing what's true without distortion or drama

- **Curiosity** – Open-minded and nonjudgmental, asking instead of assuming

- **Compassion** – Caring deeply, without rescuing or fixing

- **Confidence** – Rooted in inner knowing, not external validation

- **Courage** – Willing to act, even when fear is present

- **Creativity** – Seeing possibilities and imagining new paths

- **Connectedness** – A sense of belonging to yourself, others, and the world

The 5 Ps that Support the 8 Cs

These reinforce and express Self-energy in action:

- **Presence** – Fully here, right now

- **Patience** – Allowing things to unfold without force

- **Perspective** – Seeing the big picture, not just the problem

- **Persistence** – Staying with it, especially when it gets hard

- **Playfulness** – Tapping into joy, lightness, and experimentation

When your pursuit is rooted in these qualities, you are not chasing success from fear. You are embodying it from fullness. You're not just pursuing the goal. You're embodying the kind of person who can enjoy it, sustain it, and lead from it.

Once I saw that clearly, things really started to change. I began to notice a direct connection between my experience of time and the energy I was operating from. Almost every time I felt rushed, depleted, scattered, or behind, I realized I was not in Self-energy. I wasn't calm. I wasn't clear. I wasn't connected. I was in fear, in proving, in pressure.

So, I began using this as a compass. Before I took action, I would pause and ask: *Am I moving from one or more of the 8 Cs or 5 Ps?* If the answer was yes, I knew the time spent would nourish something real, even if the outcome didn't go as planned. If the answer was no, I paused. I recalibrated. I returned to Self before moving forward.

You can spend ten hours hustling from scarcity and still end the day feeling empty. I've done it more times than I care to admit. You check everything off the to-do list and somehow still feel unaccomplished.

But when you move from connection, when clarity or creativity or courage fuels your effort, time begins to stretch. The work flows. It feels meaningful. Even rest feels sacred instead of guilty. Slowness feels wise instead of wasteful.

What became clear for me is that it's not just about how much you do. *It's about who you are while you're doing it.*

When you shift your relationship with time, everything starts to feel different. You stop treating it like a race you're losing and begin to see it as the container where your real life happens. Time becomes less about getting through the day and more about being *in* the day, on purpose, on fire, and fully alive.

You stop measuring success by how much you got done and start asking: *Did I feel present? Did I feel connected? Did I feel lit up by what I gave myself to today?*

That's when the pursuit becomes sustainable, because you're no longer living to outrun the clock. You're creating moments that matter. You're pouring your energy into things that ignite you, and *that's* the kind of life that doesn't burn you out. It builds you.

One of the simplest but most powerful practices I give my clients is to start noticing when you're in *time prison* versus *time freedom*.

Time prison sounds like:
- I'm already behind.
- There's not enough time.
- I shouldn't have wasted that hour.
- I can't afford to rest.
- I should be further.

Time freedom sounds like:
- I have enough time to do what matters.
- How I use this moment is my choice.
- Time spent in Self-energy is never wasted.
- I trust the rhythm of my life.
- The process is the point.

Feel the difference? One makes you shrink. The other helps you expand.

I still use this practice constantly. I use it while writing this book, while running my business, and while planning my social calendar. When I catch myself getting tense about deadlines or to-dos, I pause and ask: *Am I writing from clarity and creativity? Am I connected to the heart of this chapter? Or am I just trying to rush something out of urgency?*

When I'm spending time with the people I love and feel the magnetic pull of productivity whispering to check my phone, I ask: *What does presence look like right now? What would it feel like to be here, fully?*

When I'm planning my week and my calendar looks like a jigsaw puzzle, I ask: *Which of these things can I approach from curiosity, courage, or joy? Where do I need to create space so I can bring my whole self, not just my body, to the room?*

This isn't about perfect time management. Life will still be full. There will still be seasons where things move fast, and days when everything feels like a lot. That's not failure. That's reality. The practice is learning to notice the energy you're moving from in the midst of it all. And when you can name it, you can shift it.

You begin to reclaim time not by bending it to your will, but by anchoring yourself in a different relationship to it. You stop measuring your worth by the number of boxes you checked and start measuring it by the depth of presence you brought. You stop chasing the illusion of *"caught up"* and start building a life that feels alive.

What you eventually realize is that you will never *"catch up."* There will always be more to do. The to-do list is like one of those old-school cloth towel dispensers in public restrooms. Remember those? You would pull on what looked like the end, hoping for something clean and complete, but more would just keep coming.

Life is like that. You pull on the list, and more appears.

Here is the part most people miss. If you are constantly trying to *get through* your day, you are also *getting through* your life. You are rushing past the moments that matter. You are missing the actual experience of being here.

So many people live on autopilot, believing that peace, freedom, or joy is waiting for them on the other side of the list. But there is no finish line where everything is done and life suddenly begins.

Whatever you think is waiting at the end—rest, presence, fulfillment, fun—you don't have to wait for some arbitrary point of completion to have it. You get to access it now.

The point is not to race through the day and finally arrive at living. The point is to live while the day is unfolding. Your life is not something to finish. It is something to feel.

Your life is the endless cloth towel. You do not need to get through it. You need to be *in* it.

The point is not to master time like a machine. The real invitation is to master your relationship with time. When you do, no matter how full the day or how long the list, you remain fully yourself. You stay present. You stay grounded. You stay free.

That is time well spent.

And just so we're clear, I'm saying this to myself as much as I'm saying it to you. As I edit this very section, I'm managing my own mind around a totally arbitrary deadline I set to have all the edits done by Monday.

Why Monday? Because somewhere in my head, I've linked that date to the belief that if I finish by then, I'll get to enjoy more time, more freedom, and more ease in the days that follow.

But here's what I know. None of that is waiting for me on the other side of a finished to-do list. The clarity, creativity, fun, presence, and *"maximized"* experience I think I'll earn once the edits are done are actually all available to me *right now*.

I know it's not the deadline that creates my experience. It's my thoughts. And the more I stay connected to that truth, the more time opens up, and so do I.

Compass Check:
- Where in my life am I relating to time as an enemy instead of an ally?
- Where am I moving from scarcity and urgency rather than clarity and Self-energy?
- What thoughts about time are no longer serving the version of me I am becoming?
- How can I build more moments of presence, patience, and perspective into how I move through time this week?
- What would it feel like to pursue from trust in the process instead of fear of falling behind?

Be It Now: The Everyday Practices of Living Free

Here's where it gets real.

You've made it through the chapters. You've looked at your patterns, some for the first time. You've stood in front of the mirror and chosen to stay instead of escape. You've questioned the beliefs that were quietly shaping your life and rewrote the ones that no longer serve you. You've made space for your emotions instead of bypassing them. You've restructured your support system, simplified your path, and started practicing what it means to sustain your own freedom.

You've done the deep work. You've remembered truths your soul always knew but life taught you to forget. Now the question is simple, but it's everything:

Are you ready to live it?

The pursuit isn't about landing one big, shiny moment. It's not about achieving a goal you could point to and say, *"There. That's where I became free."* The real pursuit is about coming home.

When my husband and I first started dating and talked about our hopes for life and love, he asked what I wanted in a relationship. My answer was, *"I want to go home."* (Yes, I actually said that out loud. I was only slightly surprised that he didn't run for the hills after that woo response.)

I didn't mean a physical place. I meant a way of being. I wanted to feel safe enough, known enough, whole enough to be fully myself.

What I've come to realize is that relationships, like most things in life, are classrooms. They bring up our splinters and old wounds to help us find our way back to ourselves. Coming home isn't about another person or perfectly lined-up accomplishments. It's about remembering who you already are and learning how to move through the world as your whole, aligned, fully expressed Self—not someday, but today.

This is where the pursuit becomes lived. But be careful. That high-achieving, goal-chasing part of you is probably already trying to turn this moment into another finish line. That part wants to measure how well you're embodying the material. It wants to score your progress, prove your mastery. It wants to wait until everything feels perfect before giving yourself permission to say, *I am free.*

Don't fall for it. That's Arrival Addiction wearing a new outfit, disguised as self-improvement.

What I've come to understand is that there is no final arrival. There's no test to pass, no ultimate level to unlock where the pursuit ends and perfect living begins. There's only this moment, and your choice inside it.

The pursuit was never a destination. It was always a way of being.

If you take nothing else from this book, take this: You do not need to get *"there"* to be free. You need to be free in how you walk *there.* The point was never the outcome. The point is who you become while you move toward it. The point is how you live while you're still living.

Maybe when you first opened these pages, you believed freedom lived on the other side of something–perhaps a launch, a relationship, a body, a bank account, a level of success, a sense of belonging.

Maybe you thought freedom was a reward for having done enough, healed enough, achieved enough.

But you know better now.

Freedom isn't a finish line. It's a practice. It's a way of being that you either embody, or you don't. And the best time to embody it is right now. You're never going to feel fully ready, so stop waiting. You don't need your nervous system to be perfectly regulated, or your inbox to finally be empty, or for your inner critic to go silent.

Now is the time, even in the midst of all the mess and momentum, all the grace and grit.

If you're not being it *now,* you won't magically become it *later.*

This is where your optimal blueprint becomes your guide. Earlier, we talked about the inner compass of the 8 Cs and 5 Ps. That's not just cute alliteration. That's your map. It's your alignment. It's the energetic fingerprint of your capital-S Self: calm, clarity, curiosity, compassion, confidence, courage, creativity, connectedness, presence, patience, perspective, persistence, and playfulness.

When you're connected to these energies, you stop striving from scarcity. You stop performing to prove. You start creating from sufficiency. You start moving from trust. You lead with integrity, and you show up with your soul intact.

A couple of years ago, I was approached by two business partners who wanted to bring me in on an expansion of their company. The idea was to create a new offer for their audience using my coaching expertise. On paper, it looked like a perfect fit. The opportunity made logical sense. My brain was nodding *yes*.

But when I paused and checked in with presence, curiosity, and clarity, my gut gave me a different answer. Something in me knew it wasn't right. It didn't feel expansive. It felt tight, off, misaligned.

At the time, I couldn't fully explain why I was saying no. It didn't make sense to my mind, but it made sense in my body. And later, as more details surfaced, it became crystal clear why that path wasn't meant for me.

That's what it looks like to live free, not just in the big dramatic decisions, but in the everyday practice of choosing alignment over obligation. Instead of outsourcing your choices to logic, pressure, or external validation, you learn to anchor into your inner knowing. That's where your highest wisdom lives. And when you honor it, the path that serves your highest good, and the good of everyone involved, starts to reveal itself.

You might be wondering, *How do I actually know when I'm in my optimal blueprint? What does that feel like in real life?*

That's where the practice begins. This isn't about chasing perfection or nailing it 100% of the time. It's about building an intimate relationship with your own signals. This is about learning your own energy, noticing when you're in it, when you're not, and how to return to it.

So, pause with me here. Close your eyes if it helps. Reflect on the following questions.

- When do you feel most like yourself?
- When do you feel grounded, alive, and lit up, not in a performative way, but in a way that feels deeply true?
- What sensations live in your body when you're operating from alignment? Is it a quiet steadiness? A creative buzz? A sense of spaciousness or sacred connection?

There is no right or wrong answer. This is *your* blueprint. This is the signal you return to again and again. The more familiar you become with it, the easier it becomes to notice when you've veered off course, and to gently recalibrate.

Now, for all my reluctant participants out there, I see you. I *am* you. I know this can sound soft or unnecessary. Believe me, I love a solid to-do list and a productivity hack as much as anyone. But I've also learned that this subtle inner work is powerful. This is what allows me to actually experience the life I'm building, instead of just racing through it. This is the difference between my deepest fear I mentioned earlier (that I'll create a beautiful life and somehow miss it) and the grounded joy of actually living it while it's happening.

So how do we bring this into daily life? How do we anchor into our blueprint, shift our mental state, and take fulfilling, soul-aligned action?

Let's get into it.

Start with the Mind
The S.T.E.A.R. model (Situation, Thought, Emotion, Action, Result) remains one of the most grounding tools I teach (see Chapter 4 for a full walkthrough). Every experience you have flows through this sequence. When your mind is on autopilot, old scripts take over and your pursuit gets hijacked by fear or conditioning. But when you become aware, you reclaim authorship.

Each morning, take five minutes to run a mental scan:

- What situation is most present in my mind today?
- What thought am I having about it?
- What emotion is that thought generating?
- What action is that emotion likely to fuel?
- And what result will that action create?

Then ask yourself:

- Is that thought helping me create the life I actually want?
- Is it aligned with who I'm becoming?
- If not, what thought would serve me better here?
- What emotion do I want to feel as I move through today?
- What action would that emotion naturally lead me to?

It doesn't need to take an hour. It just requires intention.

Ground Yourself in Your Optimal Blueprint
From there, ground yourself in your optimal blueprint. Before the notifications start buzzing, before you open your email or dive into tasks, pause and ask:

- What energy am I choosing to bring into this day?
- Which of the 8 Cs or 5 Ps do I want to embody in my pursuit today?
- What does that feel like in my body, my breath, my posture?

Build in Micro-Moments
Then build in micro-moments throughout your day to check in. You don't need to stop your world. Just pause for 10 seconds at a red light, in the bathroom, or in between meetings.

Ask:

- Am I being the person I want to be right now?
- What would alignment look like here?
- Which quality do I want to access in this moment?

Weekly Reflection
And when the week comes to a close, don't just move on. Reflect.

- Where did I feel free this week?
- Where did I fall back into old patterns?
- What pulled me off center?
- What helped me stay grounded?
- What is one shift I want to make as I move into next week?

These aren't just reflections. They're recalibrations and realignment in real time.

The Power of Celebration
Whatever you do, don't skip celebrations. Your nervous system needs to register joy, satisfaction, and freedom as safe. It needs to get familiar with what success actually feels like, not just in outcomes, but in your body. So celebrate the moments you showed up differently, when you honored a boundary, when you protected your energy.

Let those wins land.

This is how you expand your capacity for enough-ness. This is how you build a sustainable pursuit. It doesn't happen through shame or hustle.

It happens through presence, grace, and a deepening trust in who you're becoming.

Let It Breathe

And please, don't grip this process too tightly. Let it breathe. Let it dance.

Yes, pursuit is sacred. Yes, embodiment matters. But don't forget to play. Don't forget to laugh at the old parts of you trying to micromanage your growth. Don't forget that this gets to be human, messy, and deeply alive.

Let your life be an experiment in freedom. Let the pursuit be a playground, not a punishment.

What I've learned is that there is no final destination. You'll walk this path again and again. *See → Shift → Stay → Structure → Simplify → Sustain.* Each loop will bring new awareness, deeper freedom, and more joyful alignment. And that doesn't always feel great. That's not a problem. That's what becoming looks like.

So stop waiting to feel ready once you get there. *The path is the becoming.*

Be it now.

Be the person you're becoming. Be the one who walks into the room with shoulders back, chin lifted, not out of ego, but because you've stopped apologizing for taking up space. Order that latte with confidence (*grande, extra hot, two shots, thanks*), set boundaries without overexplaining, and laugh fully without checking to see if it's too loud.

Move through the world like you know you belong. Let your energy walk in first, calm, open, and steady. Make eye contact. Don't shrink when it gets uncomfortable. Breathe before you respond. Let your silence speak when words aren't needed, or speak up when they are, even if your voice shakes.

Let freedom show up in the small, ordinary things. Close your laptop at 5:00 p.m. without guilt. Have a dance party and karaoke moment while you're cleaning the kitchen. Catch yourself spiraling and choose to step outside barefoot instead. Let yourself cry when it's honest, rest when you're tired, and laugh even when the to-do list isn't done. Give perfectionist thoughts a skeptical side-eye when they try to sneak in and steal your freedom.

Let the pursuit be the point.

You're no longer chasing something because every step forward is fulfilling or purposeful. This isn't about waiting until it's all figured out. It's about practicing the life you actually want, starting now. *You, my friend, are already free.* You are simply learning how to live like it. And this is just the beginning.

Compass Check:
- Where am I already embodying freedom in my everyday life?
- Where am I still waiting to "get there" before I let myself feel free?
- What is one small choice I can make today to practice being the person I am becoming?

Chapter 11:

The Sacred Mess of Becoming

Permission to Be in Process: Owning the Sacred Mess

I wish someone had told me earlier that the mess is not a mistake. It's not proof that you're failing. It's not the part you're supposed to clean up before you're allowed to be proud of yourself.

The mess *is* the process. It is holy ground.

But that's not how most of us are taught to see it, is it?

This is especially true for those of us who are wired for high achievement (you know who you are). We're raised on gold stars and clean report cards. Raise your hand if your report said something like *"gets good grades but talks to her neighbors too much."* We learn early that polish gets praised, that performance earns belonging, and that the world is quicker to celebrate the people who make it all look effortless than to honor those in the raw, messy middle of figuring out who they are.

So we adapt. We smile. We succeed. We learn to tie our worth to how put-together we appear. And for a while, it works... until it doesn't.

It's all fun and games until one day you wake up successful but suffocating.

Then you begin the deeper pursuit, the kind we're doing here, and realize that the very strategies you used to feel safe are now the ones you need to let go of.

Nobody warns you that when you start walking toward a life that's true, free, and deeply aligned, it will bring up everything that *isn't*. Turns out, that's not a glitch in the system.

That *is* the system.

When you begin telling the truth about what matters to you, and when you stop abandoning yourself for applause or approval, things shift. As you start choosing your own voice over the voices that shaped you, you will meet all the parts of yourself that were taught not to.

You will come face-to-face with fear, perfectionism, trauma, and scarcity. You will stumble into old stories you didn't even know you were still living. You'll notice your body tightening as you step into new rooms. You'll hear the ghost-voices of authority figures, teachers, parents, culture, whispering, *"Who do you think you are?"* You'll catch yourself shrinking in moments you thought you'd outgrown.

And this is where most people want to quit, because we've been taught to equate difficulty with doing it wrong. The story goes, *If I were really healing, if I were really aligned, this wouldn't feel so vulnerable. I wouldn't be crying on the bathroom floor. I wouldn't be triggered. I wouldn't still be dealing with this.*

But that's a lie.

What I've discovered is that if you're doing it right, it will feel real, raw, and sometimes rowdy.

Sometimes, real is hard. You are not improving yourself. You are becoming more fully yourself. That kind of transformation doesn't come wrapped in neat bows. It comes with unraveling. It comes with molting.

Think about a snake shedding its skin. Think about a crab between shells. In that in-between space, the creature is soft. It is exposed. It is tender and vulnerable, but it is also growing. It has outgrown the old. It cannot return.

And neither can you.

The shedding is not a sign that something's wrong. The shedding is evidence that something sacred is happening.

I used to believe that the more I healed, the cleaner and straighter my path would look. That the more I learned, the less often I'd get triggered. That the more self-aware I became, the less I'd ever doubt myself.

But that's not what happened.

What happened was that the more I healed, the braver I became. The braver I became, the bolder I acted. The bolder I acted, the more edges I met. And those edges woke up deeper fears, more tender parts, and old grief I hadn't yet allowed to surface.

When I left my full-time job to go all in on my coaching business, I expected to feel empowered and free, and I did. But I also felt exposed in ways I hadn't anticipated.

I thought I had worked through my fear of failure. I thought I was past the need to prove myself. But suddenly, every social media post, every offer I made, every empty calendar day stirred up that old inner voice: *What if this doesn't work? What if you're not enough? What if people stop listening?*

And don't even get me started on the mental drama that came up when I'd look at the number (or lack thereof) of people listening to my podcast.

But none of this meant that I had failed at growth and healing.

It's a both/and. I had grown in many ways, and there were more areas for growth, evolution, and healing.

It meant I had grown enough to reach a new edge. That edge brought with it the next layer of work, the kind of work that wasn't about fixing anything, but about *staying* with myself in the discomfort. It was calling for me to let the fear rise without letting it lead me and my decisions. It gave me the opportunity to let the grief move without letting it derail me.

That's what real healing looks like.

It's not always clean or linear. It's building the guts to keep going after what you want while feeling exposed, insecure, and wildly human. It's showing up with your full heart, even when your hands are shaking.

Or as I'm known to say, even when you're sweating in your armpits.

The path of aligned pursuit isn't a path of perfect identity. It's a path of *expanded capacity*. The capacity to meet yourself in the mess, to walk yourself through discomfort, to sit with uncertainty without reaching for the quick fix.

Real freedom grows in proportion to your tolerance for imperfection, uncertainty, awkwardness, and stretch.

If you can only feel worthy when things look good, you will limit what you're willing to risk. You will stay small enough to feel safe. But if you can learn to expect the mess, normalize it, and honor it, your capacity will stretch wider than you knew possible.

You'll become someone who doesn't confuse being uncomfortable with being wrong. You'll learn to stay instead of self-abandon. And that, my friend, will change everything.

One of my clients once told me about what she called her *"Emotional Kitchen Floor"* moment. She was in tears, again, on the same tile floor where she'd cried a year earlier, activated by the same pattern, the same fear. Her thought was, *"Here I am again. Same floor. Same tears. I must not be getting anywhere."*

But she *was*.

Because this time, she caught it. She named it. She didn't shame herself. She didn't run from it. She stayed. She wrapped her arms around the tender part of her that was hurting. She chose to lead herself through it rather than abandon herself in it.

Then she got up off the floor, fed her kids, and ran her 7-figure business.

That *is* the work. That *is* the point.

The goal isn't to avoid the kitchen floor moments. The goal is to become someone who knows what to do with herself when they come.

That's emotional maturity. That's self-leadership. That's freedom.

Another client, who had been raised to be the *"good girl"*, always agreeable, always accommodating, shared a story with me after she finally stood up to her boss.

"I thought it would feel amazing," she said. *"I thought I'd feel strong, but instead I cried the second I got in my car. I felt like I'd done something wrong. I wanted to go back and apologize."*

But she didn't.

In that moment, she realized something powerful.

The tears weren't a sign she had failed. They were the voice of the younger version of her who had never been allowed to speak. The pain she felt wasn't the cost of doing it wrong. It was the price of doing it right, for the first time.

That's what healing often feels like. We think it will feel euphoric, but usually, it feels tender, new, and honest.

This is what I mean when I say the mess *is* the process. So let me give you permission, right here and now:

Let it be messy.
Let your voice tremble.
Let your action be imperfect.
Let your grief surface.
Let yourself fall apart sometimes.
Let yourself wobble.
Let yourself come back stronger, because you didn't push the feelings down. Instead, you walked through them and made it to the other side.

You do not need to *perform* the pursuit. You are allowed to *live* it. People won't respect you less for being in process. They'll trust you more. And even if they don't, you will.

That matters more than anything.

Here's a metaphor I often use. The process of becoming is like learning to ride a bike without training wheels.

At first, you overthink every movement. Your shoulders tense. You grip the handlebars like your life depends on it. You waver. You tell yourself, *"I should be better at this by now."* You might fall. You might get scraped up. You might want to put the training wheels back on, just to feel steady again.

But you can't find balance by staying still.

You find it by wobbling forward.

Every shaky start, every imperfect pedal, every overcorrection, it's all teaching you something. Slowly, subtly, the fear gives way to flow. One day, you look up and realize you're riding. Maybe not perfectly at first. But you're riding, free of the training wheels.

All because you didn't skip the part where you wobbled.

That's becoming.

It will feel clunky before it feels graceful.
It will feel vulnerable before it feels powerful.
It will feel like regression before it feels like growth.

That doesn't mean you're broken, incapable, or doing it wrong. It means you're practicing. It means you're on the path.

So, remember this. The goal isn't to master the process of becoming. The goal is to increase your capacity to *stay with yourself through it*, and to *love yourself in it*.

The goal is to keep showing up continuously, with softness and courage, even when it's hard to see the vision of who you're becoming.

You don't have to do it all at once. But you *do* have to stay. You *do* have to keep choosing presence over performance, grace alongside grit, and self-permission over self-punishment.

Yeah, grit's part of it, but not the white-knuckle, push-through kind. The kind that says, *"This matters, and I'm not abandoning myself to get there."*

The paradox is that the more permission you give yourself to be in the process, the more powerful your presence becomes. You'll trust yourself more. You'll lead yourself better. You'll soften without collapsing. You'll stretch without snapping.

You'll build a deeper kind of freedom that can't be taken, because it was never performative to begin with.

That is the sacred mess of becoming. And it is the soil where your truest self will grow.

Where You Really Came From: Reclaiming Your True Identity

Let me tell you about a reclamation moment.

I was back in Iowa visiting. Already, the trip felt charged. There's something about returning to the landscape of your becoming that awakens a thousand little echoes. The air smells familiar, but you're not the same. Everything is both deeply known and strangely distant. Every trip home carries that quiet friction between who you were and who you've become.

On this particular visit, I made a decision. It was a simple decision on the outside. But inside, it landed like a tectonic shift. The decision was that I wouldn't make the extra two-hour drive to visit my mom. I was managing a dozen moving pieces, trying to be faithful to my own energy, my own limits, and my own rhythm.

I chose what I needed that day.

That may not sound radical, but for someone raised in the shadows of guilt, obligation, and caretaking, it was monumental.

Then I got a message: *"I guess you forgot where you came from."*

That sentence. That one line. It slammed into my chest like a fist wrapped in all my old training.

If you've ever tried to break free from a version of yourself that was shaped to keep the peace, you know how sharp a comment like that can feel. It carries an entire weight of implication. *You're ungrateful, selfish, disloyal.* They're the kind of words that poke at the tender places inside you.

I could feel the pull instantly. The reflex to shrink, scramble, explain, make it right. I felt the tug to perform repentance in order to prove I was still the good one.

But something else stirred too.

A different voice rose beneath the familiar guilt. There was a deeper knowing. It was a voice I'd been learning to trust, slowly and steadily, over the course of my own pursuit. It whispered something solid, something still:

I haven't forgotten where I came from. In fact, I finally remember.

And I don't mean a small town in Iowa. I don't mean the family roles I was trained to fill, like the responsible one, the strong one, the fixer, the quiet carrier of everyone else's chaos. I don't mean the lineage of addiction or the echo chamber of dysfunction I was born into.

That's not the deepest truth.

I came from the Creator. I came from Source. I came from Love. That is where I really come from.

That is what shaped me before anything else had the chance to. That is the ground I stand on now.

I am not the outcome of someone else's decisions.
I am not the product of generational wounds or codependent dynamics.
I am not the mask I wore to survive.
I am not who I was told I had to be in order to belong.

I am a creation of something holy.

And no one gets to rewrite that truth.

These are the moments that test you.

The more you pursue a life that is aligned, the more resistance you will meet from the stories that want to keep you small.

This doesn't happen because people are cruel. It's because the shape you're becoming no longer fits the mold they're used to.

Sometimes the resistance shows up as a side comment. Sometimes it arrives as guilt disguised as love. Sometimes it lives in your own head, disguised as self-doubt or second-guessing.

But it all boils down to this. The world will try to pull you back into who you used to be. It will ask you to stay digestible, familiar, and unchanged.

That's when the real practice begins.

You have to learn how to let people be wrong about you. That's real self-leadership. It's not correcting, contorting, or convincing. It requires being, breathing, and standing rooted in who you *know* yourself to be.

It's one of the hardest things you'll ever do… and one of the most liberating.

Most people never realize how much of their identity was handed to them by family, culture, or early survival strategies. It becomes so internalized that it starts to feel like the truth.

But if you want to live free, you have to start asking better questions.

What if who you are is not who you were told to be?
What if identity isn't something inherited, but something claimed?
What if the life you want doesn't require rejecting your history, but simply choosing not to be defined by it?

In Pursuit Insight:
You can honor where you come from without reliving it. Loving your family doesn't mean repeating their patterns. That's *part* of your story but it doesn't have to author your future.

This is where so many people get stuck. They're terrified that shedding the old roles means severing love or betraying their people. But it's not betrayal. It's maturity. It's agency. It's clarity. You are allowed to outgrow old containers, even ones that kept you safe for a while, perhaps especially those.

You're not here to live out someone else's version of who you are. You're here to live yours. When you start doing that, when you start stepping into what matters to you, identity triggers will rise from others and from within. Old roles will whisper. Familiar guilt will knock. This is why I teach something called identity resilience. It means staying anchored in your truest Self, even when the emotional tide tries to pull you back.

When the fear surfaces or the projections come, pause and ask:

- Is this voice speaking from love or fear?
- Is this about my true identity or my inherited one?
- Is this pulling me into alignment or out of it?

Then return to the truth.

I came from Source. I came from Love. I came from something bigger than this moment.

The more you practice this, the freer you become. You stop needing approval. You stop contorting to stay palatable. You stop trying to earn your own belonging.

You realize you already belong to yourself, to something greater, to the essence of who you are beneath all the noise.

Your nervous system will start to tell the truth before your mind catches up. You'll feel peace where there used to be panic. You'll recognize self-abandonment not as your fault, but as an old habit you're ready to release. And over time, like a muscle being worked, your truth will hold.

The first time you hold your ground in the face of guilt, it will feel shaky. The second time, less so. The third time, you'll surprise yourself.

Eventually, you'll just live from that truth, without explaining it to anyone. It won't come from rebellion or pride. It will come from clarity.

You'll be able to say, *"That's your story about me. It's not mine."* and mean it, with love.

This is the real work of becoming. It's not just about healing the past. It's about claiming the future. It's choosing to carry forward what's true and life-giving and setting down what no longer belongs to you.

This doesn't mean you have to cut people out of your life for not understanding you or your path. It's about cutting the cord that says their understanding is required in order for you to walk it.

Freedom doesn't always look like distance. Sometimes, it looks like redefining what you're willing to carry, and who you're willing to become, without waiting for permission.

You don't need to wage war against your origins. You don't need to disown your story.

But you *do* get to decide how you carry it. You get to choose what it means. You get to write a version that honors both the beauty and the breaking, without being defined by either.

I remember watching this made-for-TV movie as a teenager. I couldn't even tell you the title now, but there was a scene I've never forgotten. A girl was finally telling her boyfriend the truth about her birth, that she was the product of rape. She looked at him and said, *"Now you know who I am."*

And he looked back and said, *"No. That's where you came from. It doesn't define who you are."*

Cue the waterworks.

And not just from the screen. Teenage me was sitting there, silently carrying a secret of my own. It was a secret shaped in a house with addiction. That story carried a lot of shame. I never told anyone, not even my closest friends. Beneath it lived a belief I hadn't yet questioned. It was a belief that said: *Because of where I came from, I was somehow damaged, defective, or less than.*

That one line cracked something open. Maybe I could write a different story.

You can love the people who shaped you, and you can still refuse to live from their limitations.

You can see your past clearly and still choose a different future.
That's not rejection. That's reclamation.
That's what it means to honor yourself.

Someone once asked me what the best advice I've ever gotten was on the subject of self-expression and identity.

I pulled out my phone and opened the Notes app where I've kept little fragments of truth from teachers I love, Thich Nhat Hanh, Michael Singer, Oprah, Brené Brown, Deepak Chopra. And I read them out loud:

- You are not your thoughts. You are not your past. You are the awareness that holds all of it. You are free.
- You are responsible for the energy you bring into the room, not the energy projected onto you.
- Your true identity is not defined by your body or your family. You are a field of infinite possibility.

- Your alignment is your power. The more you return to your true Self, the less you'll need external validation.
- You're not here to spend your one wild life proving you're worthy of it. You already are. Live like it.
- You are worthy of love and belonging, not because you've earned it, but because you exist.
- Your story does not diminish your worth. It is the birthplace of it.
- Nothing real can be threatened. Nothing unreal exists.

That list is my lifeline and anchor. When the noise gets loud, when the world tries to define me by what I've lived through, I come back to it, and I remember.

I know where I come from.

And I get to choose who I become.

Lead Yourself Through the Mess

By now, you've probably picked up what I'm laying down about personal growth. It's not linear. It's not polished. It's not a curated Instagram highlight reel of breakthroughs and glow-ups. It's messy. It is gloriously, inconveniently, disorientingly beautiful… and so very messy.

This is why one of the most important skills you will ever build in pursuit of a life that feels aligned, alive, and truly yours is the ability to lead yourself through that mess. The goal is not just to survive it. The goal is to lead yourself through it with grace, grit, and self-trust.

And yes, I do mean *skill*. Leading yourself through the sacred, unscripted, unpredictable middle of transformation is not something most of us were taught.

We were taught how to follow rules, how to keep the peace, and how to pursue goals with clean bullet points and five-year plans. We weren't taught how to stay anchored when the path dissolves under our feet. We weren't taught how to keep walking when the map is gone and the old identity no longer fits, but the new one isn't solid yet.

That's what this section is about.

What I've learned is that if you don't learn how to lead yourself through the mess, you will sabotage your pursuit. You'll bail when it gets hard. You'll collapse when the fear spikes. You'll fall back into old patterns and call it "wisdom," when really, it's just self-protection.

But when you build the capacity to stay with yourself, even when it's shaky, and you learn how to walk through uncertainty without abandoning your values or your Self, you become unstoppable. You stop performing and start embodying. You stop outsourcing your leadership to coaches or partners or circumstances. You start leading from within, and that is what makes the pursuit sustainable.

So, let's get practical.

If we don't name what the mess actually looks like, you'll keep mistaking it for failure. You'll assume that discomfort means you're doing something wrong. But the mess is not the enemy. The mess is the evidence of movement.

It usually starts subtly. You hit resistance. You second-guess decisions you already made. You feel like a beginner again, and your high-achiever self absolutely hates that. Emotions like fear, doubt, grief, longing, and shame begin to rise, louder than you expected and more persistent than you planned for.

Your identity wobbles. You catch yourself thinking, *Maybe I'm not cut out for this. Maybe I'm doing it all wrong. Who even am I right now?*

Your nervous system sounds the alarm. Even if you're logically safe, your body feels like it's in danger. You feel the familiar tug of the old life calling you back because it's predictable, quiet, and doesn't require you to stretch outside your comfort zone.

That is not failure.

That is the Sacred Mess. The Messy Middle. Or what I sometimes call the River of Misery. It's that strange, in-between place where you've left the safety of the familiar but haven't yet landed on solid ground. You're between who you were and who you're becoming. You're between the stories you've outgrown and the new ones you haven't quite built yet.

Your system does not like this liminal, in-between space, so it rebels, resists, and contracts. That's normal.

The mess itself isn't the problem. The real question is: *How will you lead yourself through it?*

In every sacred pursuit, whether you're writing a book, launching a business, healing your relationship, or becoming the next version of you, you will experience phases of expansion and contraction. You'll have moments where you feel unstoppable and moments where you can't remember why you started.

Often, the messiest moments won't be because of external obstacles. They'll be internal.

They'll come when an old identity is crumbling, and a new one hasn't taken root yet. They'll come when the same protective patterns you swore you were done with show back up.

They don't resurface to punish you. They're here to ask: *Are you sure you're ready for more?*

What the Mess Looks Like
Let's name what that might look like.

Maybe it's **identity regression**: you find yourself reacting like a younger version of you when the moment is calling for your growth.

Maybe it's **emotional dysregulation**: your old tools feel out of reach, and you're edgy, anxious, overreactive.

Maybe it's **relationship whiplash**: people in your life subtly or not-so-subtly pushing back against your growth with guilt trips, withdrawal, or criticism.

Maybe it's **success guilt**: you hit a milestone, and instead of joy, you feel shame, undeserving, anxiety, dread.

Maybe it's **nervous system fatigue**: after weeks of "holding it together," your body simply says, no more.

Maybe it's a **full-blown spiral of self-doubt**, wondering if you're actually cut out for the life you say you want.

So, what do you do when these moments come? How do you stay in the pursuit without collapsing back into the safety of your old self?

Let's walk it through.

Four Steps to Lead Yourself Through

1. Spot the Regression Without Shame
First, notice the pattern. Pay attention to when you've slipped into an old pattern. And whatever you do, don't shame yourself for it. If you can see it, that means you have awareness which means you're already leading. Old patterns will rise. That's part of healing. That's part of expansion. What matters is that you notice them and choose consciously how to respond.

In Pursuit Insight:
The point is not to avoid the mess. The point is to become someone who can walk through it with grace, grit, and deep self-trust.

Ask yourself:

- What part of me is running the show right now?
- Is this my grounded, Self-led energy, or a scared younger part?
- What does this part need? Can I bring compassion instead of judgment?

That practice alone, spotting the pattern without spiraling into shame, can shift everything. It keeps you out of the spiral of *"why am I back here again?"* and puts you back in the seat of choice.

2. Double Down on Nervous System Anchoring
When you're in the sacred mess, your nervous system will light up like a siren. You'll want to retreat, lash out, over-explain, or overwork. This is where we apply the "state before situation" principle. This is a self-leadership tool that reminds you to regulate your internal state before trying to manage the external situation.

Most of us are conditioned to react. When something activates us, like a text, a deadline, a setback, or a difficult conversation, we jump straight to fixing, explaining, proving. But when you respond from a dysregulated state, you create more chaos, not clarity. Your inner compass shuts down. Your creativity shrinks. You default to survival mode.

Instead, anchor first. Find safety in your body before taking action. That might look like:

- Ten slow breaths with a long exhale
- Shaking out your limbs for two minutes
- Walking outside with no phone
- Journaling to clear the mental static
- Placing your hand over your heart and saying, *"It's okay to be here. I've got me."*

These aren't luxury practices. These are leadership tools. They're how you shift your state so when you do act, you're doing so from Self, not panic.

3. Protect the New Identity

One of the trickiest parts of the sacred mess is that it can feel like an invitation to abandon the new identity you've been building. The mess will try to convince you to shrink, backtrack, and question whether the new identity you're stepping into is too much. You'll start to think, *"Maybe I'm not ready. Maybe I'm faking it. Maybe this version of me won't be accepted."*

This is where identity scaffolding becomes essential. These are structures that help you stay connected to who you're becoming, even when it feels unfamiliar.

Your scaffolding might be:

- A daily journaling ritual: Who am I becoming? What would they do today?
- Reading your Purposefully Derived Thoughts each morning (See chapter 4 for a refresher on PDTs)
- Visual cues such as wearing a bracelet, posting a sticky note, using a lock screen that reminds you of your vision and your why
- Taking one small action daily that affirms the new identity, even if you don't feel "ready"

The point isn't to force belief. It's to stay connected to the version of you that you're choosing to become so that you don't unconsciously collapse back into the old one.

4. Stay With Yourself When You Most Want to Bail

This is perhaps the most sacred leadership skill of all. This is the part where you consciously choose to stay with yourself when every part of you wants to hide, disappear, and abandon your dreams. Your job is to lead yourself through it by whispering, *I'm not going anywhere*, when your mind says, *This is too much*.

Ask yourself:

- If I trusted myself 5% more, what would I do right now?
- What would love say to me in this moment?
- What does staying with myself look like right now?
- What does this scared version of me need to hear right now?

Sometimes the answer will be rest. Sometimes it will be action. Sometimes it will be calling a friend, drinking water, crying it out, or breathing through the fear. It doesn't matter what the action is. What matters is that you take the action *with* yourself, not *against* yourself.

There was a time when I hit a shiny success milestone in my business. On the outside, it looked like a total win. On the inside, it felt like a total mess. I experienced a wave of insecurity. Enter all the sneaky thoughts: *What if I can't sustain it? What if I let people down? What if I was fooling everyone? What if it's a fluke?*

And oh, did I want to disappear. My brain served up its favorite old playlist: play small, downplay the win, shrink, blend in. For a hot second, I was tempted; but here's the thing. I've done this work. I knew this was the sacred mess talking, not the truth. So, I pulled out the tools. I anchored my nervous system. I breathed. I came back to my body. I remembered who I was becoming, and then I took the next aligned step.

Did I have to magically erase all the fear first? Nope. I just had to stay with myself and walk through it. That's what leading yourself through the mess looks like. You don't wait for it to feel perfect. You don't hustle to outrun the doubt. You just stay in the room with yourself long enough to keep moving forward, one aligned choice at a time.

The pursuit isn't linear, and the process of becoming is anything but tidy. But your capacity to lead yourself through the sacred mess is the real flex. That's what turns the whole pursuit into true freedom.

When you can stay with yourself even when it's messy, wobbly, and uncertain, you no longer fear the next level of growth. When you trust that you can walk yourself through whatever comes, you no longer fear what's on the other side of your next expansion or opportunity.

That's not just resilience. That's freedom.

Compass Check:
- Where do I tend to abandon myself when the pursuit gets hard?
- What's one small practice I can use to anchor myself the next time I feel wobbly?
- How would I move through this next stretch if I fully trusted who I am becoming?

Chapter 12:

WARNING: Side Effects May Include Joy

▍Manifesto of Pursuit

I am not here to perform life.
I am here to live it. To feel it.
To experience all of it, the fire and the fog,
the joy and the grit, the stretch and the stillness.

I do not chase goals to prove my worth.
I pursue them to know myself more fully,
to meet the parts of me that only awaken when
I leave the comfort zone of certainty and
step into the wild unknown.

I am in pursuit, not of perfection, but of presence.
Not of applause, but of aliveness.
Not of gold stars, but of sacred truth.

I reject the myth that success lives at the finish line.
I know the destination will always feel like the journey,
so I choose to make the journey feel like
freedom, fun, and fulfillment now.

I do not wait for peace, purpose, or permission.
I create them.

I allow rest to be strategic. I let play be productive.
I choose compassion over critique, courage over control,
and joy over judgment.

I refuse to abandon myself just to get somewhere faster,
because the most important thing I will ever arrive at
is me.

I am not imprisoned by pursuit.
I am ignited by it.
I am not just chasing a dream.
I am becoming the version of me
bold enough to live it.

This is what it means to be in pursuit.
And I've got me from here.

As you read that Manifesto, I hope you noticed what stirred, what felt like home, what made you pause, breathe differently, or sit up a little straighter. I also hope you noticed what felt slightly uncomfortable, like something you're not used to claiming but secretly long to.

That's the power of a Manifesto. It isn't meant to be tidy. It's not a final draft of who you've become. It's a living, breathing declaration of what you are choosing to pursue. It's a proclamation that you may not have all the answers, but you're willing to stand for something true.

Later in this chapter, I'll invite you to write your own. It doesn't have to be poetic or long. It just has to be yours. I'll invite you to write a few sentences or a page that captures the values, commitments, and ways of being you want to carry into your pursuit. But for now, just let the idea land. You'll come back to it soon.

Living From the Inside Out

There's something wild that happens when you start living your life from the inside out. The first shift is subtle. You might notice a softness, a steadiness, or a strange and sacred sort of clarity. Things that used to rattle you suddenly don't hold the same charge. People who used to intimidate you start to feel human again. The rules you followed without questioning begin to dissolve.

It's not that you stop caring. It's that you start caring differently. You care more deeply, from your center rather than from a need to prove or perform.

This shift doesn't come because you've floated into some dreamy land of "good vibes only." You're still fully here, awake, and human. But something inside you re-roots. And when that happens, everything else begins to reorganize around that deeper center.

When you pursue a life that is aligned to your own values, led by your voice, your truth, your internal compass, the world can swirl and spin as much as it wants. You no longer reach for external noise to tell you what matters. You already know. You've chosen what to hold, what to release, what to create. You've become someone who knows what is and isn't yours to chase, fix, explain, or prove.

That's what makes the pursuit sacred.

It's not that it becomes neat or predictable, but it demands something honest from you. It asks questions that tug at the soul, like:

Who am I becoming?
How do I want to move through this world?
What kind of life do I want to experience?
If I'm going to be on this spinning globe, in this human flesh suit for a finite amount of time, what is it I want to do with my time, energy, talents, and curiosities?

Those are the real questions. And most people are too busy running a race they don't even choose to ask them. They're living from the outside in, hustling toward goals they don't remember why they wanted. They're performing versions of themselves that were built for approval, not alignment. They're measuring success by metrics that drain them and checking boxes that once made sense but haven't fit in years.

They're drowning in "shoulds" handed to them by someone else's fear. Their days feel like stages, and their life starts to blur into a performance that is unexamined, relentless, and unsatisfying.

No wonder so many people feel numb, bitter, or restless. No wonder joy feels scarce, and peace feels expensive. They're chasing applause in rooms they don't even want to be in.

But when you start living from the inside out, you stop needing the performance.

You start remembering your own damn life.

Let me be very clear: this isn't about rejecting ambition. I'm not here to glorify chaos or tell you to ditch structure and float into the abyss. I love a good calendar. I love clear goals and showing up for them.

It's about re-rooting your pursuit in what actually lights you up, fulfills you, and grows you, instead of chasing metrics that will never deliver what they promise.

If that sounds easy, it's not. It's work, but it's the right work.

You can't hustle your way out of misalignment. It doesn't matter how many late nights you pull, how polished your presence looks, or how generous your captions are. If you're building a life from the outside in, you will eventually collapse beneath the weight of what you've created, because you didn't build it to hold you. You built it to hold an image. And that never works. Not for long.

You might reach all your milestones and still feel like something's missing. You might earn the applause and still feel hollow, because applause cannot give you purpose, and admiration cannot give you peace. Validation might stroke the ego, but it will never satisfy the soul.

So here's the invitation. It's not a command or a formula. It's a tender, open-handed invitation:

Build from the inside out.

You get to lay down the question, *"What will they think?"* and pick up the question, *"What do I want to create with my life?"*

That's when everything shifts. You don't need the world to validate you before you take a step. You stop needing the algorithm, the inbox, the bank account, the body, or the relationship to prove your worth. You start living in pursuit of something quieter and truer, something that might not trend on TikTok but feels like oxygen in your lungs.

Imagine building a stunning house on quicksand. You hire the best team, you style it perfectly, it sparkles with every detail. From the outside, it's impressive. It gets compliments. People want to be invited in. But deep down, you know the truth. The foundation is sinking. And every day, you wonder if it will hold. That's what building from the outside in feels like.

But when you build from the inside out, everything changes. You take the time to pour the concrete and lay the stone. You get quiet and ask, *What do I actually need? What matters to me? What kind of life would I want to wake up in, not just show off?*

It might take longer. It might not look flashy at first. It might even feel lonely while the world is chasing trends and you're tending to your roots. But slowly, the structure rises. Slowly, your life begins to feel like home. When storms come, as they always do, you're not scrambling to patch a façade. You're anchored.

The most magnetic people I know are the ones who stopped performing and started embodying. You can feel it. You sense their energy before they say a word. They are not living to impress. They are living to express. They don't need applause because they're not waiting to be chosen. They already chose themselves.

I'll never forget the day I got to meet one of my mentors in person. Yes, I had to pay what felt like the price of a used car to spend a single day with her in her Austin penthouse, but it was worth it for one reason alone. I got to witness firsthand what it looks like when a woman is fully embodied.

She walked into the room like she was greeting old friends, not strangers off the internet. There was nothing performative about her presence. There was no trying or striving. When she spoke, when she moved, when she taught, it all came from a grounded, rooted place. She wasn't putting on a show. She was simply sharing herself, her wisdom, and her work with us. And you could feel the difference.

That's the energy I want for you. That's the energy I want for *me*.

I'm not talking about a shinier version of your life or another thing to chase. I'm talking about a deeper, new way of *being* in the world.

Being *In Pursuit* is a posture, mindset, and relationship with your life where *you* are the one who decides what matters and how you want to pursue it. When you live from that place, life starts to feel alive again… even the messy parts… even the slow seasons… even the moments that don't look impressive on social media.

You start to *want* your life, and that freaking matters.

Confession of a Woman in Pursuit

There is a particular kind of discomfort that signals you're standing at the edge of your own evolution. It doesn't always scream. Sometimes it hums, low and persistent, like a frequency only you can hear. For me, that edge is here, right now, in the quiet, pulsing truth I'm about to admit.

I'm pursuing a revenue goal in my business—a big one.

There. I said it.

Even typing that out, my fingers hesitate. My breath catches in my chest, like my body has been conditioned to hold still at the moment of truth. There's an old, familiar uneasiness that stirs just under the surface— a flutter in my belly, a flush of heat in my cheeks. The part of me that still craves invisibility whispers, *Keep that tucked away. If no one knows, no one can question it. No one can question you.*

But hiding keeps you stuck, and I've spent too many years editing myself into what I thought was acceptable.

The stories I've carried about money are not casual. They're generational. They're deep-in-my-DNA kind of stuff. I didn't pick them. I inherited them. They've lived in the background like static, always there, murmuring, shaping how I see the world, even when I'm not paying attention.

Good people don't care about money.
Wanting wealth is greedy.
If you make too much, you'll lose touch. You'll lose your softness. You'll lose the people who loved you before.
You'll become someone others resent. You'll become someone you don't recognize.

These whispers are the residue of scarcity narratives I didn't ask for but absorbed anyway. They're not rooted in truth, they're rooted in survival. And that's exactly why this goal matters.

This revenue goal isn't about what I'll buy, though yes, I have vivid, life-giving plans for how this money will support my family, my mission, my rest, and my work in the world. But more than that, I care about who I have to become to hold this kind of wealth with integrity, sufficiency, and joy. I'm not chasing a dollar amount. I'm chasing a kind of wholeness I've never fully allowed myself to claim.

This isn't about accumulation. This is about transformation.

It's about letting go of old armor, the kind built from scarcity-soaked beliefs, inherited scripts of self-denial, and identities shaped in the crucible of shame. It's about freeing myself to step into a new relationship with worth, value, visibility, and contribution. I want my insides and outsides to match. I want the life I'm building to reflect the healing I've done and the healing I'm still doing.

I was not raised to believe this was safe, or even possible. I was raised on cautionary tales and clipped coupons. On *"Money doesn't grow on trees,"* and *"You shouldn't want too much."* On silent glances when the topic of wealth came up, like it was impolite to want more than enough. That the people who did were selfish, disconnected, and a little suspect.

In my field, social work, this narrative was canon. Service meant sacrifice. Integrity meant invisibility. We wore burnout like a badge of honor and judged anyone who dared to price their work in alignment with its impact. I can still hear the well-meaning comments: *"It must be so hard to charge that much."*

Translation: *Don't forget where you came from. Don't be one of those people.*

But growth has a way of unraveling what no longer fits, if you let it.

Over the past few years, I've raised my prices. I didn't do this out of ego or greed. I did it out of alignment, and, if I'm totally honest, after a lot of coaching on it. Every time, I was terrified. I braced for judgment, for the silent exits, for people to walk away and confirm my worst fear, that wanting to thrive meant I was abandoning my integrity.

But what happened shocked me.

Clients didn't disappear. They came closer, with more commitment, more resonance, and more readiness for the kind of transformational work we were doing. Something shifted in the energetic exchange. It felt cleaner and more honoring. It was no longer an offering extracted from self-sacrifice. It was a mutual agreement rooted in value and belief.

A turning point for me happened when I agreed to speak at an event for a discounted rate. I loved the people organizing the event and really wanted to be part of it. After the event, the coordinator handed me an envelope. Inside was a check for my full speaking fee. She looked me in the eye and said, *"Don't ever discount the value of your services."*

That moment hit hard. It felt like the Universe was saying, *This is what happens when you stand in your worth.* I realized that the people who are truly aligned with you won't ask you to shrink. They'll meet you with honor, support, and encouragement. They'll celebrate your prices, not question them. They'll gladly invest in the transformation you help create.

So now, I'm setting my sights on a new milestone. Again, this is not a declaration of greed. It's an act of reclamation, a practice of healing, and a statement that doing good and doing well are not in conflict.

My husband has a T-shirt in his company that says, *"You can be both."* It's simple, but it's a whole sermon. You can be both wealthy and generous. You can be both grounded and rising, heart-led and well-compensated. The idea that we have to choose is the lie.

This is the new story I'm choosing to live.

I'm choosing one that says integrity and abundance are not opposites, and that you can be fully expressed and fully resourced at the same time. This is a conscious uncoupling from the belief that smallness is virtuous. I am choosing to believe that my enough-ness is not contingent on staying broke, burnt out, or behind the scenes.

The resistance still comes. Of course it does. The thoughts still visit. They say things like, *It's not polite to talk about money. You're making people uncomfortable. You're not the kind of person who can have that much. Who do you think you are?*

And every time they arise, I name them. I breathe. I remind myself that these are ghosts, not gospel. They are echoes of a system designed to keep good people small. I don't need to fight them. I just need to keep choosing something different.

What excites me most about this pursuit isn't even the number, it's the unfolding. I'm captivated by the invitation to become someone I haven't fully met yet. I'm ready to step into the version of me who doesn't dim or defer, who doesn't need to justify wanting more for herself, her family, or her community.

I know I'll have to let go of the identity of *"the poor kid from the wrong side of the tracks."* That story served me for a long time. It helped me feel grounded, relatable, and good. But it's not who I am anymore, and it's certainly not who I want to keep becoming.

I'll have to release the belief that I'm not capable enough or strategic enough to steward this level of success. I'll have to strengthen a new muscle around being seen and learning to speak about the value of my work with clarity, confidence, and joy. I'll have to continue building my capacity to receive abundance as a reflection of alignment, not arrogance.

I don't know exactly what traits or skills will surface along the way, but I trust they will. That's the nature of aligned pursuit. It reveals you to yourself. It draws out dormant capacities and invites you to embody them. It shapes you from the inside.

I want to reach this goal not just with a fuller bank account, but with a fuller self, more generous, more grounded, and more free.

This pursuit is not happening in isolation. In other areas of my life, I'm also consciously practicing what it means to pursue with alignment and intention.

Case in point. I've somehow convinced myself to sign up for a couple more races, half marathons this time. (Don't worry, no more full marathons for this girl. That chapter is closed.)

The goal isn't about performance or comparison. It's about honoring my body, my strength, and my resilience. Training gives me something to focus on that connects me back to myself in a tangible way. I like having a reason to lace up my shoes and get outside. I like the conversations with running buddies about training plans, fueling strategies, and how to schedule long runs around life, work, and unpredictable weather.

It's weirdly fun.

And, surprisingly, I've started to enjoy the challenge of seeing if I can improve my time. I'm not what I'd traditionally call "competitive," but there's something satisfying about watching myself grow stronger and more capable with each run.

It's not about chasing a finish line. It's about becoming someone who shows up, consistently, intentionally, and with joy.

After a knee injury from running a full marathon this past spring, this goal feels different now. I'm approaching it gentler and wiser. It's no longer about pushing through pain or proving something. It's about listening. It's about partnering with my body instead of demanding from it. It's about giving it the care, rest, and reverence it's always deserved.

Yes, this is still a pursuit of endurance. But it's also a pursuit of tenderness.

That same energy is showing up in other parts of my life, too. I'm in pursuit of deeper nervous system regulation. Years of inner work have gifted me the ability to recalibrate after I've been activated. I know how to pause, reflect, and recenter. But now, I want to stay grounded in the first place.

The goal is progress, not perfection. Instead of 0–10 reactivity, my goal is 0–8, then 0–6, and maybe eventually 0–2. I don't need serenity at all times. I just want more presence to it. I want to be in my life as it's happening, not constantly recovering from it.

Another area that feels like a continuous DIY project is my relationship with worthiness. I'm still learning the quiet courage it takes to release those old deficiency stories, the ones that try to slip back in every time I stretch into something bigger. The whispers are sneaky:

You don't belong. You're not smart enough. You're too much. You're not enough. You're out of your league.

They don't shout anymore, but they haven't gone silent either. And every time I meet a growth edge, I meet them again.

They're old friends now, familiar, but no longer trustworthy. Every time they show up, I have a choice. I can let them lead, or I can meet them with compassion and keep walking toward the version of me that's waiting on the other side.

The work I do in the world is about this very process. I help people recalibrate their focus to see what is already within them, and to access it in ways that allow them to show up more intentionally, gently, and purposefully in their lives.

I do this work because I believe in the inherent worth and wisdom of every person I encounter. And I want my own life to reflect the same truths I help others remember.

Pursuing a revenue goal is not a departure from my values or this work, it is an embodiment of them. Just like training for races and doing the inner work to challenge my old deficiency stories, this goal is part of a larger commitment.

I am committed to living what I teach.

I want to pursue freedom, fulfillment, and aligned success without apology. I want to show that it is possible to move toward something with purpose instead of pressure. It is possible to hold both ambition and compassion.

You can challenge yourself to grow in new ways without abandoning your self-trust. This is what it looks like to honor your wholeness, to move forward with your heart, your body, your truth, and your dreams fully present.

This is what it means to be a whole human in the process of becoming. This is what it looks like to live in pursuit. And this is your invitation, too.

Let your goals stretch you. Let your dreams stir things up. Let your pursuit be imperfect and alive and deeply human. You don't need to justify it. You don't need to shrink it. You don't need to know exactly how it's all going to happen. You only need to begin.

And remember, the side effects may include joy.

Close the Book, Go Live It

This is the part in most books where things tie up in a tidy bow. The music swells. The camera pans out. A final page turns, and you're left with the clean satisfaction of something complete. But this isn't that kind of story, and I'm not that kind of author.

There is no bow. No curtain call. No closing credits rolling over a happily-ever-after. Because this isn't the end. It's the beginning.

This book was never meant to be a destination. It was meant to be a doorway and a starting line. It's an offering that says: here, take this spark, and now go light the fire.

If you came looking for a polished conclusion, I hope instead you find a lived permission slip. One that says your pursuit doesn't need to be tidy, linear, or certain. It just needs to be yours.

What you've been reading isn't a summary, it's a summons. It's a quiet but resolute voice, nudging you to listen to the truth you've likely known for a long time. Something in you is ready. It's calling for a shift, a stretch, or an adjustment to live from the inside out.

You didn't pick up this book because you lacked information. You've read the books. You've listened to the podcasts. You've sat in the seminars, scribbled the notes, and highlighted the quotes. You know the formulas. You know the hacks. Insight isn't what's missing.

What's missing is often the one thing we can't download or outsource—permission. Permission to want what you want. You actually don't need my permission, but I'm going to give it to you anyway.

You get to admit it out loud, whatever "it" is for you. You get to want joy without justifying it. You get to want success without shame. You get to stop performing life and finally start inhabiting it. You came here not to be taught, but to be reminded of your power, your depth, and your truth.

You came here to explore the terrifying, liberating possibility that you don't have to choose between your ambition and your alignment. That your success doesn't have to cost you your soul, and your pursuit doesn't have to be a performance.

You came here because something in you is tired of circling the same questions, and is ready to live into the answers. You came here because a quiet part of you is ready to come home.

And if I've done my job, I hope you're walking away with this one anchoring truth:

The real point of any pursuit is not the finish line. It's who you become while you're still running.

The goal isn't to finally arrive at a version of yourself that is flawless and finished. The goal is to let the process shape you so wholly, so honestly, that you begin to taste wholeness on the way there.

And here's the magic. When you stop chasing wholeness and start living like you're already worthy, the results come faster. And even when they don't, you're no longer waiting to feel alive. You're already alive.

You laugh more, breathe more, risk more, and play more. You create from sufficiency rather than scarcity, from curiosity rather than fear. You live your life, not just perform it. And you realize that fulfillment was never waiting at the end. It was always in how you pursued the goal.

So now, my invitation to you is this:

Close the book and go live it.

Let this be the moment you stop waiting for the perfect plan or the perfect version of yourself to emerge before you take action. Let this be the moment you choose movement over mastery. You don't need to have all the answers. You just need a willingness to begin.

If your brain resists or your stomach flips, that's normal. Gag and go if you must. Take one breath. Take one bold (or shaky) step. Ten seconds of courage, that's all that's ever required.

And when you inevitably wobble, because you will, come back to your Manifesto.

Reread it when your brain floods with doubt. Let it remind you of the truth that exists deeper than the fear. Speak it out loud when you feel small or uncertain. Let it interrupt the story that says you're behind or broken or too late. Let it anchor you when the world feels loud and your fear gets noisy. Let it be your compass, your cue, and your call back to what matters most.

If you haven't yet written it, now is the time. Don't wait until you feel ready, or when you have more time, or when the fear is gone. Do it now. Let it be messy, raw, and honest. Pin it to your wall. Save it on your phone. Tape it to your mirror. Read it on the days you forget who you are and what you're here for, because you will forget. You're human.

But the more you return to it, the more quickly you remember.

Write Your Manifesto of Pursuit

This doesn't need to be long or polished. It just needs to be true to you, to this moment, and to the life you're choosing to create. Use the prompts below to guide you. You can write a single sentence, a bold declaration, a list, or a full page. There's no wrong way to begin.

- What do I want to stop performing in my life?
- What do I want to start pursuing, from a place of presence and alignment?
- How do I want to feel while I pursue my goals?
- What values do I want to embody as I move forward?
- Who am I becoming through this pursuit?
- What do I want to remind myself when the old stories and fears resurface?
- What does success mean to me now, not just at the finish line, but in how I live along the way?

Your Manifesto is a living document. Let it evolve as you do. Start with what is true today. Speak it out loud. Return to it often.

The First Step

You don't need to change your whole life in the next thirty days. You don't need a five-year plan, or a mood board, or a miracle morning to qualify. You just need to choose one thing. Choose one pursuit, one bold, aligned, maybe-a-little-scary goal that calls to the version of you you're becoming. Write the first line of that chapter. Make one small decision that moves your life in the direction of your own becoming.

Check in with yourself weekly. Get curious and ask:

Where am I pursuing from presence?
Where am I still performing?
Where can I soften or stretch or take the next small step?

You don't have to do it all. You just have to do something in the general direction of your goal. And if you want support for that journey, if you're ready to live this pursuit more fully, with more courage, clarity, and joy, coaching is one of the most powerful tools I know.

Coaching isn't about fixing yourself. You were never broken. It's about becoming on purpose. It's about having someone beside you who sees the real you, calls you forward, and holds space for your power and your mess with equal reverence. It's about truth-telling and story-shedding and soul-aligned strategy.

If that's what you're craving, I'd be honored to walk with you. You can learn more about working with me at jessicasmarro.com.

Whether we ever work together or not, the most important thing is this. *Go live it.*
You've read enough. You've learned enough. You've prepared enough. You've waited long enough. Now is the time to live what you know.

You don't need permission. You already have it.
You don't need a guarantee. You just need to go.
And I'll be right here, on the pursuit path with you.

So, close the book. Go live it. The world needs what only you can bring.

Your Next Chapter Starts Here

You've done the inner work. You've walked through the prison, the path, and the pursuit. Now let's keep the momentum going, together.

Scan this QR code to access your personalized Next Chapter Hub where you'll find:
- My direct contact info & social links
- New free resources you won't find in the book
- Access to book a *free Pursuit Consult Call* with me
- Early invites to workshops, retreats, and coaching opportunities

This isn't goodbye. This is the doorway. Come on in.

References

Castillo, Brooke. "About Brooke." *The Life Coach School.* Accessed
    August 3, 2025.
    https://www.thelifecoachschool.com/brookecastillo.
Dana, Deb. *The Polyvagal Theory in Therapy: Engaging the Rhythm of
    Regulation.* New York: W. W. Norton & Company, 2018.
Hanson, Rick. *Hardwiring Happiness: The New Brain Science of Contentment,
    Calm, and Confidence.* New York: Harmony Books, 2013.
Neff, Kristin. *Self-Compassion: The Proven Power of Being Kind to Yourself.*
    New York: William Morrow, 2015.
Porges, Stephen W. *The Polyvagal Theory: Neurophysiological Foundations of
    Emotions, Attachment, Communication, and Self-Regulation.* New
    York: W. W. Norton & Company, 2011.